North Wales

Although every effort is made to ensure that all information printed in this guide is correct and up to date, Michelin Travel Publications (a trading division of Michelin Tyre PLC) accepts no liability for any direct, indirect or consequential losses howsoever caused so far as such can be excluded by law.

CONTENTS

Introduction	5
Geography	6
Historical notes	6
Language	16
Welsh Cuisine	17
Sights	19
Isle of Anglesey	20
Bala	25
Bangor	26
Barmouth	28
Beaumaris	30
Betws-Y-Coed	32
Blaenau Ffestiniog	34
Bodelwyddan	36
Bodnant Garden	37
Caernarfon	38
Chirk Castle	41
Colwyn Bay	42
Conwy	43
Denbigh	46
Dolgellau	47
Elan Valley	48
Erddig	51
Harlech Castle	54
Holyhead	56
Knighton	58
Llanberis	60
Llandudno	62
Llangollen	66
Llanwrtyd Wells	72

Lleyn Peninsula	73
Machynlleth	78
Montgomery	79
Newtown	80
Penrhyn Castle	81
Plas Newydd, Anglesey	82
Plas Newydd, Denbighshire	83
Porthmadog	84
Portmeirion	86
Powis Castle	88
Rhuddlan Castle	91
Rhyl	92
St Asaph	93
Snowdonia	94
Tywyn	103
Valle Crucis Abbey	104
Lake Vyrnwy	105
Welshpool	106
Wrexham	107

Practical Information — 109

Planning a Trip	110
Getting there	110
Motoring	111
Places to Stay	111
What to buy locally	119
Visiting	119
Sport	120
Further reading	121
Calendar of Events	122

Index — 123

INTRODUCTION

■ Geography

The principality is approached from the east via the English **Marches**, attractive farming country interspersed with hill ranges anticipating the mountains beyond. The gentle swelling forms of the sheep-grazed uplands of Mid-Wales contrast with the drama of the mountains of **Snowdonia**, true highlands of great grandeur. To the west extends the remote Lleyn Peninsula. The narrow coastal plain of North Wales abounds in seaside resorts. Offshore across the Menai Strait is the Isle of Anglesey.

■ Historical notes

Prehistory: c 24000 BC to AD 78

Stone Age – The headless skeleton of a 25-year-old man provides the earliest evidence of human life in Wales. It was found in Paviland Cave, on the southern Gower Peninsula, where its ritual burial probably took place in about 24 000 BC.

Bronze Age – From about 1800 BC gold, copper and bronze work was introduced into Britain by the Beaker People, named for their practice of burying earthenware pots with their dead in single graves. Stone was still in wide use.

Celtic Tribes – The Celts first settled in Britain c 1000 BC, having spread from central Europe through the Mediterranean and into Asia Minor. While the Goidelic Celts inhabited Ireland, the Brittonic branch moved into England and Wales, bringing with them sophisticated bronze-working and farming skills. Modern Wales can trace its language and elements of its culture back to the Celtic age, which lasted well over a thousand years.

Wales under the Romans: AD 78 to 5C

Claudius, the Roman Emperor, successfully invaded Britain in AD 43 and by AD 76-78 the western Celtic tribes were under attack. Anglesey, headquarters of the Druids, was conquered in 78, despite the spirited resistance of painted women, who screamed at terrified troops across the Menai Strait. Military bases, linked by long roads, were set up in **Caernarfon**

(Segontium), **Chester** *(Deva)*, **Brecon** *(Y Gaer)* and **Caerleon** *(Isca)* to control western territory. On the whole, Celtic life continued undisturbed and many leading families were integrated into Roman society. Some British leaders, such as Magnus Maximus, known in Welsh as Macsen Wledig were even granted a measure of autonomy.

Post-Roman Invasions: 5C to 11C
As Roman troops began to withdraw in the 5C, Britain became the target of a series of new invaders. Goidels from Ireland and Picts from Scotland threatened the British Celts from west and north, and Anglo-Saxons swept across the south and east. The Brythons, confined to the western mainland, now began to refer to themselves as *Cymry* (meaning "fellow countrymen") – still the Welsh name for its people; the Anglo-Saxons knew them as "Weleas", or "foreigners" or possibly "the Romanised people".

Missionaries – With the Irish invaders came Christian missionaries *(sancti)*. Previous attempts to convert the pagan Celts had met with little success: the Roman missionary, St Augustine, apparently offended local chiefs by remaining seated when they were presented to him. The *sancti* had more of an impact and were even granted parcels of land – the *llan* of many Welsh placenames – on which to establish a network of churches and monasteries. One of their number, born in Pembrokeshire in the mid-5C, became the patron saint of Wales, **David**, *Dewi* in Welsh.

Welsh Kings – During the 5C a powerful dynasty was established by Cunedda Wledig in north and west Wales, while other royal houses, possibly of Irish descent, emerged in the southwest. Wales was divided into several principalities, including Gwynedd, Powys, Meirionydd, Ceredigion, Dyfed and Gwent. Each one was a separate political unit, though on the whole they coexisted peacefully. Unity came only with the new threat of the Vikings, the Norsemen, who began their attacks on Britain in the late 8C. By this time three Anglo-Saxon kingdoms had evolved: Wessex in the south, Mercia in the midlands and Northumbria in the north. In 784 Offa, King of Mercia, marked the boundary between his territories and those of the Welsh with a ditch, **Offa's Dyke** (167mi/269km long), which still more or less defines the English-Welsh border.

By the 9C the Vikings had settled in northern Britain and Ireland and on the Isle of Man but they were kept out of Wales by **Rhodri Mawr**, Prince of Powys, who extended his rule through marriage to take in most of the Welsh lands. Nevertheless, while the Anglian (English) kingdoms of the east were developing into a single political power during the 9C and 10C, Wales could not sustain a unified system. The Welsh practice of gavelkind *(cyfran)* – sharing territory between all sons – ensured the division of Rhodri's inheritance into six princedoms, all of which submitted to Alfred, the English king.

Deheubarth – Rhodri Mawr's grandson, **Hywel Dda** (Hywel the Good) built up a new empire, uniting the southern territories into the Kingdom of Deheubarth (south-west Wales) and extending his rule to Gwynedd and Powys. He advocated the policy of living at peace with the English and of paying tribute to the men of Wessex. He too, however, was forced to accept the supremacy of the English throne; he died in 950. His main achievement was to collect and codify the laws and customs of Wales to form a legal system which lasted until the 13C.

Normans and Welsh Uprisings: 1066 to 1485

Hywel Dda's death was followed by a return to confusion and sporadic internal warfare, leaving the country vulnerable to Norman incursions. William of Normandy, having led his troops to victory against King Harold in 1066, rewarded his closest associates with lands along the Marches (borders) of Wales. The Marcher lords made several inroads into Welsh territory and by the 12C Powys and Gwynedd were cut off from much of the rest of Wales. Norman gains were consolidated with motte-and-bailey castles, first of earth and timber, later rebuilt in stone.

Tudors: 1485 to 1603

During the 15C England was torn apart by the Wars of the Roses, a power struggle between the royal houses of Lancaster and York. In 1471 the Lancastrian king Henry VI was murdered and the throne passed to the Yorkists. The Welsh **Tudor** *(Tewdwr)* family had become deeply embroiled in the feud. Lancastrian Henry V's widow, Catherine de Valois, had married Owain Tewdwr of Anglesey, and their grandson, Henry, now became the Lancastrian claimant. After 14 years in exile in Brittany he returned in 1485, hailed by the Welsh as the new leader prophesied by their bards, and defeated Richard III at Bosworth. As Henry VII he ended the civil war by marrying Elizabeth of York and uniting the two houses, and founded the Tudor dynasty that would rule for another 118 years.

Acts of Union – Henry's son, Henry VIII, was determined to introduce a uniform political and judicial structure throughout England and Wales. His Acts of Union (1536 and 1543) abolished the Marcher lordships and allowed Welshmen full inheritance rights. A standardised English system of law courts was established and the Welsh language was excluded from all official channels. While covering the Welsh by the same law as the rest of the kingdom, the Acts created an even deeper gulf between the Anglicised gentry and the largely illiterate, Welsh-speaking lower classes. The survival of the language was in great part due to the growing influence of the church and to the publication of a Bible translated into Welsh by **William Morgan** in 1588.

Social and Industrial Development: 17C to 19C

Religion and Reformation – Henry VIII's creation of a Protestant, Anglican church, headed by the king, met with no real opposition in Wales but by the late 17C there was considerable dissatisfaction with church authorities. Most clergymen were badly educated and badly paid; many bishops were non-resident and none spoke Welsh. In the 1730s **Gruffydd Jones** of Llanddowror (1683-1761) set out to reach the illiterate populace through his system of circulating schools, teaching adults and children to read the Bible in Welsh.

The bid to win congregations with education was continued by **Thomas Charles** of Bala (1755-1814), who organised Sunday schools and founded the British and Foreign Bible Society, providing cheap Bibles. **Methodism**, which had started as an unconventional movement within the Anglican church, received fervent support in Wales, where it was led by **Howel Harris** of Trefeca (1714-73) and **Daniel Rowland** of Llangeitho (1713-90), both highly emotional, charismatic preachers. In 1811 the Methodists left the Anglican church and for the following 150 years its various Nonconformist offshoots continued to wield a strong influence among the Welsh.

Industrialisation – From the late 18C, industrialists began serious exploitation of the mineral wealth of Wales. Slate quarries, copper mines and smelting works appeared in the north

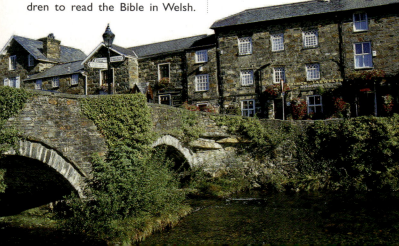

and the south, and industrial activity gathered pace during the iron boom of the early 19C. By 1827 Wales was producing half of Britain's iron exports.

Coal, originally mined for iron-smelting, was also in increasing demand, to fire steam trains and ships and to provide domestic fuel. A series of mines sunk in the South Wales valleys transformed the landscape: houses were thrown up in long terraces, eventually to be overshadowed by black slag-heaps. Despite appalling conditions, people flocked to the valleys to find work in the mines and to escape from rural poverty. Close communities were created, with the coal pits as their focus, and the valley towns became the breeding ground for a radical political culture.

Industrial barons reaped vast profits from advances in technology and transport. Railways carried coal from the valleys to new docks built by the Second Marquess of Bute at Cardiff, which grew to be the biggest coal-shipping port in the world. While coal and slate masters flourished, building extravagant homes such as **Cardiff Castle** and **Penrhyn Castle**, their workers lived on low wages, in dangerous and insanitary conditions. Riots were not uncommon: 20 people were killed in the Merthyr Riots of 1831; 28 died in Newport in 1839 during demonstrations in support of the Chartist movement for electoral and social reform.

Agricultural workers also suffered extreme hardship, exacerbated by depopulation and the imposition of toll charges on roads, discouraging itinerant trade. In the 1840s a spate of attacks on tollgates and houses was carried out by the so-called **Rebecca Rioters** – men dressed in women's clothes who usually operated under cover of night.

Politics and Education: 1800 to 1920

Political dissent and religious Nonconformity in Wales in the 19C were closely linked in opposition to the Anglican, mainly conservative landowners. Under the 1867 Reform Act industrial workers and tenant farmers were granted the right to vote and returned 23 Liberal members of parliament out of 33 in the 1868 elections. There followed a series of evictions from Tory-owned land which helped speed the introduction of the Secret Ballot Act (1872).

Wales remained predominantly Liberal until the 1920s, its most famous parliamentary representative being **David Lloyd George** (1863-1945), the member for Caernarfon Boroughs. As Chancellor of the Exchequer Lloyd George introduced a programme of social reform, which included the introduction of state pensions, and as Prime Minister he led the government during the First World War.

Disestablishment – By the late 19C the Anglican church had become an alien institution to the largely Nonconformist population of Wales. Resentment was particularly focused on the continuing obligation to pay tithes, an ancient Anglican tax. Strength of feeling was such that several violent riots broke out in North Wales, and the growing calls for change eventually led, after several false starts, to the passing of a Disestablishment Bill through parliament in 1914. In 1920 the Anglican church in Wales was disendowed and its money passed to the University, the National Library and Welsh county councils.

Demands for better educational provision had been growing during the 19C and in 1872 the first University College of Wales, funded by public donations, opened in a redundant hotel building in Aberystwyth.

Growth of National Feeling: 1920 to 1990s

As education became more accessible, new generations emerged of Welsh-speakers, schooled in English and staying in or returning to Wales to find professions. Members of this educated middle class were to play a leading part in the revival of national feeling and identity. Fears that Welsh culture would be lost altogether prompted a vigorous campaign to promote the use of Welsh in schools: one of the most energetic campaigners was **Owen M Edwards** (1858-1920), Chief Inspector of Schools in Wales, who published several Welsh-language magazines and books for children. He also founded Urdd Gobaith Cymru, the Welsh League of Youth which combined Christian and cultural ethics. In 1947 the first Welsh-language primary school was opened, to be followed in 1962 by the first bilingual secondary school, set up in the Anglicised industrial valleys of South Wales.

Political nationalism took on a more defined form after the First World War, and in 1925 the Welsh Nationalist Party was founded by a group of writers and scholars which included the poet and author Saunders Lewis. In 1998 it changed its name to **Plaid Cymru** – the Party of Wales. Its appeal was largely to the agricultural, middle classes, and its emphasis lay on the Welsh language and culture. Industrial communities, disillusioned with Liberal government, turned to the growing Labour movement at a time of declining trade and increasing unemployment. **Aneurin Bevan** (1897-1960), an ex-miner who played a leading role in the miners' strike in 1926, was sent to parliament for Ebbw Vale in 1929; as Health Minister in the 1945 Labour government he introduced slum-clearance policies and laid the foundations of the National Health Service.

In the 1960s and 1970s nationalist feeling found a new voice in the **Welsh**

© Wales Tourist Board

Language Society *(Cymdeithas yr Iaith Gymraeg)*, whose followers staged demonstrations and defaced property in the name of the language. Piecemeal changes in the law brought more bilingualism into official life, adding Welsh to road signs, forms and court proceedings. In 1993 a Welsh Language Act stipulated that the Welsh language be treated, as far as is reasonably practicable, on the basis of equality with the English language in the public sector. It also set up the Welsh Language Board *(Bwrdd yr Iaith Gymraeg)*.

Administration and Economy: 1960s to 1990s

Welsh unemployment was running at twice the UK national average when the **Welsh Office** was established in 1964, giving Wales limited executive powers. This was followed by the creation of the **Welsh Development Agency** (WDA) in 1976, to encourage new economic initiatives. Under the reorganisation of local government in England and Wales in 1974, the 13 Welsh counties were replaced with eight new units, most taking the names of ancient principalities. Another reorganisation of local government in 1997 brought the return of many of the old county divisions.

In the latter part of the 20C there was growing support for a measure of devolution. The first referendum, held in 1979 – for a separate **Welsh Assembly**, without legislative powers – resulted in a majority against.

The 1980s brought radical changes to industrial Wales: by the middle of the decade every coal pit in the Rhondda Valley had been closed. Despite notable success in attract-

ing foreign business to Welsh sites, former mining communities have continued to suffer from high unemployment and social dislocation. The granting of a Welsh-language television channel – S4C – has encouraged a boom in the Welsh film, TV and animation industries. **Tourism** is another area of economic success but there is widespread concern about its effects on rural society, and especially about the phenomenon of second homes and holiday cottages, which have changed the face of many communities, leaving some virtually deserted outside the tourist season.

In 1997 a second referendum on devolution produced a narrow majority (6 721 – 559 419 pro and 552 698 anti) in favour of the establishment of a **Welsh Assembly**. The parliamentary bill received the Royal Assent in the summer of 1998, making provision for elections to be held on 6 May 1999. The **Welsh Assembly** consists of 60 members, of which 40 are elected from the parliamentary constituencies and 20 from the five EU constituencies. There is simultaneous interpretation in Welsh and English and at present the members meet in Crickhowell House on Cardiff Bay. Discussions are in progress about the construction of a new building, to be designed by the winner of an architectural competition and erected in Cardiff, on a waterfront site looking outwards to the world.

■ Language

Perhaps the most apparent cultural division within Wales is that between Welsh-speakers and non-Welsh-speakers. During most of the 20C this corresponded to a great degree with the division between urban and rural Wales. Industrial communities in the south and south-east have tended to become Anglicised, while the farming and fishing communities of north and west Wales have remained predominantly Welsh-speaking. This situation has changed noticeably, though gradually, in the last few decades, as a revival of interest in the Welsh language has spread in the industrial towns, and as bilingual and Welsh-language institutions (such as the Welsh Development Agency, the Welsh Language Board and television and radio channels) have been established in the cities.

Most official transactions can be carried out in Welsh and equality of treatment for the Welsh and English languages in the public sector was ensured by the Welsh Language Act 1993. Many place names have reverted to their original Welsh spelling but, where there is any chance of confusion, road signs are bilingual.

At the same time, tourism has had an increasing impact particularly on the north Wales coastal towns, bringing in its wake an influx of English newcomers and encouraging the sale of rural cottages to buyers mainly resident outside Wales.

■ Welsh Cuisine

Although the Welsh food industry has played an important part in the British economy for centuries, the concept of Welsh cuisine has only very recently emerged. In the 1990s promoters have tried to make up for lost time, applying the **Taste of Wales** (*Blas ar Gymru*) accolade to home-grown products and to guesthouses, hotels and restaurants serving fresh local food in new or traditional recipes.

Seafood – The long Welsh coastline and its many rivers and lakes provide a wide range of freshwater and sea food, which is now enjoying a gradual revival after a post-war slump. Other seafood includes oysters, farmed at Pembroke and Anglesey and King and Queen scallops from the Anglesey coast. Freshwater delicacies such as salmon and sewin (a pink-skinned sea trout) are fished from the river Dee.

Meat – Lamb and beef have been a vital source of income in Wales since the Middle Ages. Until the 19C herds of sheep and cattle were regularly driven hundreds of miles from the Welsh mountains to English markets. The drovers who made these long and dangerous journeys became celebrated members of society and many of their routes can be followed and their resting places, the drovers' inns, visited.

Welsh lamb is now marketed all over the world as a lean and natural meat, while beef, traditionally overshadowed by the better-known lamb industry, has begun to profit from new promotion.

Dairy Products – A growing interest in old skills and recipes has brought new life to the Welsh dairy industry. **Caerphilly**, perhaps the most famous Welsh cheese, is creamy, white and mild; other cheeses include Llangloffan, which is red and flavoured with garlic, and Y Fenni, a type of cheddar with ale and mustard seed. ■

SIGHTS

ISLE OF ANGLESEY ★★

Anglesey, Mother of Wales – Môn Mam Cymru – is this island's motto, and many aspects of the heritage of Wales seem to be present here in concentrated form, from the abundance of prehistoric and early Christian monuments to the high proportion of Welsh-speakers. Like most islands, Anglesey retains a strong individual identity, reinforced rather than diluted by the pair of superb 19C structures – the Menai Bridge and Britannia Bridge – connecting it to the mainland across the Menai Strait. Drawn into the mainstream of national life by its position on the strategic route from London to Dublin, Anglesey nevertheless retains an air of remoteness over much of its windswept surface, parts of which recall that other Celtic land across the Irish Sea, with whitewashed cottages, sedge-sown fields and slow-moving streams.

(Ynys Môn) Anglesey – Population 69 149
Michelin Atlas p 32 or Map 503 FGH 23-24
Tourist Information Centre – Station Site, Llanfairpwllgwyngyll LL61 5UJ
☎ 01248 713 177;
Fax 01248 715 711

The island's glory is its coastline, most of it designated as an Area of Outstanding Natural Beauty; much of it is wild and dramatic, like the cliffs of Holyhead Mountain, though in other places rocky headlands shelter delightful coves and bays. The south-west coast is more tranquil, with broad sandy beaches and dune systems like those of Newborough Warren, while the banks of the Menai Strait have an almost Mediterranean atmosphere, with villas embedded in lush vegetation along the corniche-like road leading to Beaumaris.

Beaches – There are a few beaches on the east coast – Beaumaris, Penmon, Llanddona, Benllech and St David's – and very many all along the west coast.
Craft Centres – **Oriel Ynys Môn Craft gallery** *(see below)* and **James Pringle Weavers** *(LlanfairPG)*.

■ **Sights** *in rough clockwise order starting from the Menai Bridge*

Menai Strait – The channel (15mi/25km long) separating Anglesey from the mainland was once dry land. The divide between two valleys running north-east – south-west was gouged out some 20 000 years ago when the thawing ice sheet covering them released torrents of melting water. As the icecaps continued to shrink, the sea-level rose, flooding the valleys and making Anglesey an island.

Rip-tides surging up and down the Strait made the ferry crossing a hazardous affair and an undesirable obstruction to the free flow of traffic between London and Dublin via Holyhead, particularly irksome after the Act of Union of 1800. The graceful **Menai Bridge*** designed by Thomas Telford was opened in 1826. The suspension bridge (579ft/176m long) was the first iron structure of its kind in the world, its chains suspended from masonry pylons (153ft/47m high). The meticulous preparation of all the wrought-iron work included heating and soaking in linseed oil, not, as the White Knight told Alice, in wine:

*"I heard him then, for I had just Completed my design
To keep the Menai Bridge from rust
By boiling it in wine."*

On the Anglesey bank the great chains were secured by driving tunnels (60ft/18m) into the rock. The actual raising of the first chain was watched by a large crowd, the efforts of the labourers on their capstans encouraged by a fife band. When Telford raised his hat to signal success, two of the workmen were so elated that they somehow managed to clamber across the chain high above the water (590ft/180m).

The **Britannia Bridge** by Robert Stephenson was built a generation later, to carry the Chester and Holyhead Railway. It is an altogether heavier structure, monumentally Egyptian in character, guarded at each end by pairs of lions of distinctly Sphinx-like mien. The twin tracks of the railway were originally led through iron tubes, a method of construction first employed by Stephenson at Conwy, though there were difficulties enough during the period of construction.

Bryn-Celli-Ddu Burial Chamber – *A 5 and A 4080 W; after 3mi/4.8km turn right.* This passage grave seems to have been built on the site of a late Neolithic henge, a stone circle surrounded by a bank and a ditch. The internal passage, which is lined on one side by a low shelf, leads to a polygonal chamber containing a stone decorated with a spiral design. The finds from the excavations are now in the National Museum in Cardiff.

Llanfairpwllgwyngyll – This characterless village strung out along the old Holyhead Road leading from the Britannia Bridge was just one of the many places in Wales called Llanfair (meaning St Mary's) until in the 19C a tailor from Menai Bridge struck on the idea of extending its name by several syllables. The trick worked, and, even if its pronunciation and exact meaning (St Mary's Church in the hollow of white hazel near a rapid whirlpool and the Church of St Tysilio near the red cave) are not widely known, everyone has heard of **Llanfairpwllgwyngyllgogerychyrndrobwllllantysiliogogogoch**. What is more, visitors come here in large numbers, though all there is to see is the railway station with its cumbersome nameplate and a waiting room sheltering Victorian dummies rather than real passengers, a large coach and car park, and an even larger souvenir complex.

Llangefni – The county town of Anglesey stands on the island's longest river, the Cefni, no longer navigable, and on the old road to Holyhead, long since by-passed by Telford's turnpike. The town is at its busiest on market days.

Oriel Ynys Môn★ – Anglesey's fine modern **museum and art gallery** is committed not only to supporting local arts and crafts but also to presenting and explaining the island's strong identity to its visitors, who may well be greeted (in Welsh) by one of the friendly staff.

A series of imaginative displays evoke Anglesey's history, culture and environment. Deep inside a reconstruction of the Neolithic burial chamber of **Barclodiad y Gawres**, fire-lit figures may be seen preparing a horrid "witches' brew". Another scene shows the **royal court of Gwynedd** at Aberffraw with **Llywelyn the Last** *(ap Gruffydd)* sitting uneasily on the throne he was soon to lose. Other displays deal with Anglesey's agriculture, the copper mountain

at Amlwch, the rich bird life of the South Stack cliffs and the marine life of the Menai Strait. Emphasis is laid on current issues like the maintenance of Welsh language and identity in the face of contemporary pressures.

Anglesey Sea Zoo★ – *North side of the Menai Strait facing Caernarfon.* Established in what was once a lobster-export business, this is a large, varied and highly entertaining aquarium, which specialises in exhibiting the diverse marine life to be found off the Anglesey coast. As well as conventional fish tanks, the Zoo has ingenious simulations of a number of habitats complete with their denizens. There is a shipwreck, surf crashing on a beach, and a convincing re-creation of the world beneath the pier. The most spectacular of the exhibits is the great **Fish Forest**, a huge

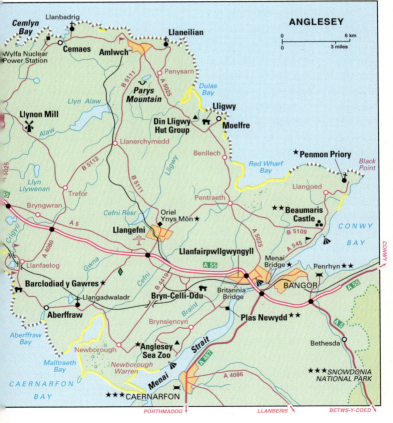

tank containing 200 000 litres of seawater; a concave window, the largest of its kind in Britain, gives onlookers the sensation of moving among the myriad fish swimming through the fronds of a growing forest of seaweed.

Newborough Warren – *It is dangerous to venture off the paths on to the mudflats at low tide.* A network of footpaths explores the different habitats of this area, one of the finest dunelands in Wales, which is now a nature reserve, inhabited by a great variety of wildlife. The forest of Corsican pine trees, which is managed for timber, was planted in the mid-20C to stop the dunes from moving; the dunes support an array of plants and insects; the estuaries and freshwater lakes provide feeding and breeding grounds for an abundance of bird life. The history of the dunes is told in the exhibition in the Visitor Centre, housed in the old Pilots' Cottages.

Barclodiad y Gawres Burial Chamber* – *Park in the car park at Cable Bay; 15min there and back on foot.* In a wonderful position on a headland overlooking Cable Bay, this is one of the most evocative late Neolithic monuments in Wales. Beneath the contours of the modern mound is a chamber reached by a passageway and flanked by smaller side chambers, all defined by upright stones, five of which are decorated with spirals, chevrons, zigzags and lozenges, some of the earliest prehistoric art to be seen in Britain. Excavation has revealed evidence of a strange event that took place at some point in the chamber's history; the preparation of a "witches' brew" made up of frog, toad, snake, mouse, hare, eel, wrasse and whiting.

Holyhead – *See p 56.*

Cemaes – *North coast.* This little resort clustering around its harbour was the chief port of Anglesey's north coast before the rise of Amlwch. Nowadays it stands between the beauty of the Heritage Coast with its splendid cliff walks and the less attractive mass of **Wylfa Nuclear Power Station** which presents a welcoming face with extensive landscaping and a lavishly equipped **visitor centre.**

Beyond the promontory enclosing the eastern side of the harbour is another headland, a wonderful site for the tiny parish **church** of **Llanbadrig**, founded, according to legend, by St Patrick in the 5C, and surrounded by its clifftop graveyard. Restoration work in 1884 – red, white and blue glass in the windows, blue glass in the east window, rare sanctuary tiles produced by a glass-making process, mosaic of the Good Shepherd in the niche – was initiated by Lord Stanley of Alderley, who had been a diplomat in the Near East and become a Muslim, and introduced some elements reminiscent of a mosque. ■

BALA

Its single street attractively lined with trees, Bala stands athwart the long south-west – north-east fault line that has long been an important communication route through the mountains between England and the Cambrian coast. Filling the deep valley to the south-west of the town is the largest natural water body in Wales, Bala Lake *(Llyn Tegid)*, its surface animated by all kinds of water sports enthusiasts in summer.

Bala Adventure and Watersports Centre – The centre organises courses (also accommodation) lasting for a few hours or several days, in a range of activities – abseiling, mountain climbing, sailing, white-water rafting, windsurfing.

Bala Lake (Llyn Tegid)* – This lake was formed in a hollow made by the Dee Valley glacier. Its gloomy waters (4mi/6km long, 140ft/40m deep) are inhabited by a unique sub-species of fish, the *gwyniad*, trapped here since the end of the Ice Age. The winds racing through the long valley between the mountains can make for exciting sailing and windsurfing. Less energetic pursuits are catered for by frequent car parks and picnic areas and by lakeside footpaths.

> *(Y Bala) Gwynedd – Population 1 922*
> *Michelin Atlas p 33 or Map 503 J 25*
> *Tourist Information Centre – Penllyn, Pensarn Road, Bala LL23 7SR*
> *☎/Fax 01678 521 021;*
> *bala.tic@gwynedd.gov.uk*

■ Excursions

Bala Lake Railway – *0.5mi/1km S of Bala by B 4391, or 6mi/10km to Llanuwchllyn by A 494 and B 4403.* The Llangollen–Bala–Dolgellau railway was closed in 1965. Part of the line has been relaid with narrow-gauge track (2ft/0.6m) from Bala Station to the railway's headquarters at Llanuwchllyn. Little steam locomotives haul tourist trains along the lakeside *(9mi/16km there and back).*

Bwlch y Groes** – *11mi/18km S of Bala by A 494, B 4403 and a minor road.* The Pass of the Cross (Bwlch y Groes) is reached by a narrow road which climbs from near the southern end of Bala Lake through the upland farms of Cwm Cynlewyd to the open mountainside. This is the highest road in Wales, offering at the summit magnificent views of the crags of the Arans *(S).* ■

BANGOR

The wattle fence around a settlement was once known as a "bangor", and the monastery founded here c AD 525 by St Deiniol took its name from the woven enclosure that originally surrounded it. Deiniol became Bishop c AD 546, making Bangor perhaps the oldest territorial diocese in Britain. Hidden from sea-borne marauders by the ridge now occupied by the University, the tiny city languished in obscurity for hundreds of years.

Growth occurred only at the end of the 18C and the beginning of the 19C, when Penrhyn slate started to be shipped out and when the Holyhead Road was completed in 1830. The University came in 1884, and Bangor today is the miniature metropolis for this part of North Wales, a busy place, especially when the 5 000 or so students are in residence.

> *Gwynedd – Population 11 173*
> *Michelin Atlas p 32 or Map 503 H 24*
> *Local map p 98*
> *Tourist Information Centre – Town Hall, Deiniol Road, Bangor LL57 2RE*
> *☎ 01248 352 786;*
> *Fax 01248 362 701; bangor.tic @gwynedd.gov.uk*

> **Craft Centre**
> The **Bangor Museum and Art Gallery** *(see below)* has a well-stocked craft shop.

Cathedral – This most modest of cathedral churches is possibly the oldest cathedral foundation (AD 525) in continuous use in Britain. It retains a few fragments of the structure built in the 12C but most of its fabric is 13C–16C, much restored towards the end of the 19C by Sir George Gilbert Scott. The cathedral's discreet location well away from the shore (like St David's) did not save it from repeated depredation by the Vikings in 1073, by King John's soldiers in 1210, during Owain Glyn Dŵr's rebellion in 1402 and from subsequent neglect.

A diminutive buttressed and battlemented belfry of 1532 stands at the western end, while the crossing is marked by a squat tower whose foundations proved to be too insubstantial to support the tall spire proposed by Scott. The interior lacks symmetry, but objects of interest include an oak carving known as the **Mostyn Christ**, a life-size figure of great expressiveness. One modern painting shows the six cathedrals of Wales in their contrasting geographical settings; another, by Brian Thomas, is a touching representation of Christ's encounter with the two people on the road to Emmaus. A "museum corner" has Flemish carvings, stone fragments and misericords.

The area around the cathedral still has a recognisably precinctual character. A **Bible Garden**, laid out in 1962, is filled with plants with Biblical connotations, like the *Cupressus sempervirens* which provided Noah with gopher wood for the Ark. The Bishop's Palace now accommodates local authority offices, and the Canonry houses the Museum and Art Gallery.

Museum and Art Gallery – This pleasingly old-fashioned museum has a Bangor Room full of local memorabilia, a Welsh kitchen, and a fine collection of 17C–19C furniture from a gentry house near Criccieth. Other furniture includes a splendid 3-tier dresser *(tridarn)* which may date from 1555; its carved inscription reads *Os yw Duw trosom, pwy a all fod i'n herbyn* ("If God is with us who can be against us"). The gallery stages temporary exhibitions.

University – In 1880 a committee set up by Gladstone recommended that Wales should have two university colleges. Aberystwyth had been founded in 1872 and Cardiff was opened in 1883 but agitation continued for an institution in the north, supported by the population as a whole, the Penrhyn quarrymen contributing a weekly deduction from their wages. The first students began their studies in 1884 in a converted inn, the Penrhyn Arms.

Bangor is a bastion of Welshness, and the University operates a bilingual policy regarding the use of Welsh and English. All official communications are in both languages, and some courses may be studied through the medium of Welsh. About 10% of the students speak Welsh as their first language.

Pier – Though never managing to turn itself into a resort as such, Bangor shared to some extent in the transformation of the North Wales coast into a holiday region. The recently reopened pier, built in 1896, seems to reach almost to the Anglesey shore of the Menai Strait. It retains nearly all its original features including the procession of charming little kiosks along its entire length (1 550ft/470m). There are fine views of the wooded Strait and of Snowdonia. ■

BARMOUTH*

This old harbour town enjoys a superlative site at the broad mouth of the Mawddach estuary. The older houses clamber up the rocky slopes which shelter Barmouth from the north, while the more modern buildings of the seaside resort are somehow crammed into the space between the splendid sandy beach and the cliff. The place became popular in Victorian times. Darwin enjoyed staying here, as did Ruskin. Today's crowds fill the beach, the promenade, the amusement arcade, or watch the varied activity around the harbour.

There is a **Lifeboat Museum**, a small local **museum** in an old house called **Tŷ Gwyn**, and, a short distance away, an odd circular **lock-up**, Tŷ Crwn, in whose constricted space men and women prisoners were somehow separated.

(Abermaw) Gwynedd –
Population 2 384
Michelin Atlas p 32 or Map 503
H 25
Tourist Information Centre
– The Old Library, Station Road,
Barmouth LL42 1LU
☏ 01341 280 787;
Fax 01341 280 787; barmouth.tic@gwynedd.gov.uk

Barmouth Bridge* – The Cambrian coast railway curves sharply through the town, then straightens out abruptly to cross this extraordinarily long bridge (2 253ft/687m) built on 113 trestles. A double span of lattice girders used to open to allow the passage of larger vessels but only pleasure-craft sail up the Mawddach nowadays. The bridge was opened in 1866. In 1980 it was closed for seven months for repairs costing nearly £2 million, its timber piling having been the

Beaches – At Barmouth and Fairbourne.
Crossing the Mawddach Estuary – The sandy spit which almost closes the mouth of the Mawddach is linked to Barmouth by **ferry** and by railway. This makes possible a trip to Fairbourne, a popular resort with a sandy beach, and a ride on the narrow-gauge **Fairbourne Railway**, returning to Barmouth by mainline train or on foot using the railway bridge.

From here north-westwards the old turnpike road has become the village's main street, lined on one side with villas and hotels. The grandest of the hotels, the *Royal Oak,* preserves in its vestibule the original inn sign painted by the Birmingham artist **David Cox** (1783-1859) who visited Betws every autumn in the 1840s and 1850s and was largely responsible for popularising the place among fellow-artists and their followers. Cox would have come here by coach, but it was the arrival of the railway in 1868 that made the village accessible to large numbers of people. Exceptionally among Welsh rural railways, the line still exists, its infrequent trains almost empty in winter, but crowded in summer with visitors exploring the rugged valley of the Lledr or on their way to the slate town of Blaenau Ffestiniog.

■ Sights

Church of St Michael – The name Betws-y-Coed signifies "bead-house (or prayer-house) in the woods" and this little 14C-15C church may be the successor to the original "bead-house". It found itself isolated from the rest of the village when the railway was built, and in 1873 was replaced by **St Mary's Church**, a far more imposing structure in sandstone, Cornish serpentine and dark local stone in a central position on the main road through the village. St Michael's is now used only occasionally but, with its rows of pews facing the pulpit rather than the altar, it remains a rare example of an Anglican place of worship unaffected by the High Church aspirations of the mid-19C. In the chancel is the effigy of Gruffudd ap Dafydd Goch, a knight who served with the Black Prince. The graveyard flanks the River Conwy, spanned nearby by an elegant little suspension footbridge, seemingly Victorian in character, but in fact dating from the 1930s.

Conwy Valley Railway Museum – A collection of mostly local railway souvenirs is housed in the museum but the main attraction is the miniature railway whose steam locomotives haul trainloads of excited children around the old goods yard of the railway station.

Betws-y-Coed Motor Museum – Among the stars in this small private collection of vintage and thoroughbred cars is an immaculate black Bugatti of 1934, an Art Deco icon of an automobile hidden for years in a Dunkirk shed after its Belgian owner had fled the German advance in 1940. ■

BLAENAU FFESTINIOG★

No place on earth quite resembles this city of slate built into the mountains at the head of the Vale of Ffestiniog. Shining from the frequent rainfall, slate IS the landscape here; the waste from the quarries, which were the local livelihood, is formed everywhere into a glittering chaos of geometric shapes apparently about to engulf the straggling settlements which make up the town. The sombre buildings appear to be made of slate, which also serves as the material for steps, fences, and for the ornaments on sale in souvenir shops. Nowadays slate extraction employs only a fraction of its former labour force but, with two quarries providing trips into the underground world of the slate miner, Blaenau Ffestiniog has to some extent succeeded in re-inventing itself as a tourist destination; it is also conveniently located in the valley between the northern and southern peaks of Snowdonia.

> Gwynedd – Population 5 349
> Michelin Atlas p 32 or Map 503 I 25
> Local map p 98
> Snowdonia National Park Visitor Centre – Unit 3, High Street, Blaenau Ffestiniog LL41 3ES
> ☎/Fax 01766 830 360

■ Historical notes

The foundations for Blaenau Ffestiniog's 19C prosperity were laid 500 million years ago, when beds of blue-grey slate were thrust upwards from the floor of the Ordovician sea. Small-scale quarrying for local needs began in the 18C, but it was in the early 19C, with the construction of William Madocks' harbour at **Porthmadog** and the completion of the gravity-powered narrow-gauge **Ffestiniog Railway**, that slate production and export began to boom. Throughout the 19C the demand for roofing slates in Britain and abroad seemed insatiable; at their height, in the 1880s, the Blaenau Ffestiniog mines were producing 139 000t of dressed slate a year and employing more than 4 000 men. Railway companies competed with one another for the lucrative traffic, forcing lines through the difficult mountain terrain. As well as the reopened Ffestiniog, Blaenau still has a mainline railway connection with the outside world via a tunnel beneath the Crimea Pass (nearly 3mi/5km long); it was built by the London and North Western Railway in 1879 and links the area with the resorts of the north coast.

Industrial disputes and the familiar British problem of absentee owners, more interested in profits and dividends than in industrial innovation, led to a steady decline in the town's fortunes. The population of the straggling settlements which make up Blaenau Ffestiniog – Bethania, Glan y Pwll, Maenofferen, Manod, Rhiwbryfdir and Tan-y-grisiau – has declined from more than 12 000 at the end of the 19C to about 5 000 today, and only a handful of workers is still engaged in extracting and splitting slate in the one mine now open to visitors.

■ Sights

Llechwedd Slate Caverns★ – Slate was found at the Llechwedd mine in 1849 and extracted until the 1970s from 16 different levels with some 250 vast chambers linked by 25mi/40km of tunnels. On the surface, visitors can explore a "**Victorian Village**", based on the old settlement of Pentre Llechwedd which somehow managed to coexist with the surface workings of the mine. As well as various shops, the *Miners' Arms* pub, a smithy and workshops, there is an exhibition **Slates to the Sea** which tells the sometimes adventurous story of the slate harbour of Porthmadog and the vessels that were built and sailed from there. One cottage, a survival from the 18C, was the home of the renowned Blind Harpist of Merioneth, David Francis (1865-1929). Also on the surface is the **Slate Mill**, with demonstrations of the seemingly simple but in fact extraordinarily dextrous skill of slate splitting. Slate is still mined here and exported to many parts of the world.

Visitors descend into the **Deep Mine** by a strange stepped vehicle running on a 3ft/900mm track at a gradient of 1:1.8, the steepest passenger railway in Britain. The train stops at Level A, but visitors descend further on foot, eventually reaching Level B, at a depth of 450ft/137m below the summit of the mountain. Here begins a tour of 10 chambers, each with a sophisticated *son et lumière* presentation of aspects of the arduous life and work of those who worked the slate in the heyday of the industry. The tour also passes through a vast lake-filled cavern.

The **Miners' Tramway,** a bone-shaking electric railway, remains on one level, but takes visitors through an equally intriguing series of caverns. Real miners demonstrate some of the wisdom and skills acquired underground, while tableaux convincingly recreate the working conditions once encountered. ■

BODELWYDDAN**

Denbighshire

Two great 19C landmarks – tall church and battlemented castle – make a decisively Victorian impact on the landscape on either side of the North Wales Expressway as it swings inland past St Asaph.

After languishing as a girls' boarding school for many years, the imposing mock-medieval castle in its parkland setting has been transformed into a wonderfully appropriate home for a superb selection of **19C paintings** from the

Michelin Atlas p 33 or Map 503 J 24

National Portrait Gallery.
The castle's striking skyline of turrets and battlements crowns the rising ground south of the main road. Built in stages in the course of the 19C, the present edifice encases parts of an earlier 16C or early-17C house purchased c 1690 by Sir William Williams, Speaker of the House of Commons, though a house is known to have stood here as early as the mid-15C.

The architect responsible for the major part of the 19C work, carried out c 1830-44, was Joseph Aloysius Hansom, inventor of the Hansom cab.

The east front is imposing, the north even more so; it has a niche with the sinister figure of Y Gŵr Hir ("Long Man") as well as a formidable arch, above which rise turrets concealing chimneys from the earlier house. Beyond the twin towers of the gatehouse a curtain wall runs west, turning the corner and leading to new buildings which form part of a hotel. ■

© Wales Tourist Board

BODNANT GARDEN**
Conwy

Italianate terraces, a deep romantic dell and magnificent mountain views make Bodnant one of the most appealing late-19C to early-20C gardens in Britain.

The estate called Bodnod on the east bank of the Conwy valley was bought in 1874 by Henry Pochin, an industrial chemist who had made his fortune in Manchester. Pochin gave what had been a typical Georgian house its present, assertive neo-Tudor appearance, then indulged his passion for conifers, planting up the deep Dell with a variety of trees which have become the superb specimens of today. His grandson, the second Lord Aberconway, was a passionate gardener of a different kind; active here until his death in 1953 and in touch with many of the eminent plant hunters of the day, he intro-

Michelin Atlas p 33 or Map 503 I 24 – 8mi/13km S of Conwy by A 55 and A 470

duced many rhododendrons, filled up the Dell with moisture-loving plants, and created the series of terraces stepping down from the house with their glorious prospect of Snowdonia. Both Henry and his son Charles were at the centre of horticultural life in Britain, serving as Presidents of the Royal Horticultural Society and in many kindred capacities. Bodnant's place at the forefront of many gardening developments has also been due to the efforts of another dynasty of plantsmen; since 1920 three generations of the Puddle family have supplied the place with its head gardeners. ■

25 miles to conwy

CAERNARFON***

Welsh through-and-through today, Caernarfon was founded as an English bastide, one of the walled castle towns built to secure Edward I's hold on North Wales. As much a palace as a citadel, its spectacular castle overlooking the Menai Strait was intended to be the focal point of the new principality, a fitting residence for a future Anglo-Norman Prince of Wales. Its ornamentation was correspondingly elaborate, while its grandiose walls and angular towers recall those of Imperial Constantinople.

The more modest fortifications of its dependent town are still intact, enclosing a grid-iron of streets laid out by Edward's surveyors in the last years of the 13C. Perhaps more than anywhere else in Wales, historic Caernarfon evokes the long centuries of Anglo-Welsh intimacy; in 1911, and again in 1969,

> Gwynedd – Population 9 695
> Michelin Atlas p 32 or Map 503 H 24
> Tourist Information Centre – Oriel Pendeitsh, Castle Street, Caernarfon LL55 1SE
> ☎ 01286 672 232;
> Fax 01286 678 209; caernarfon.tic@gwynedd.gov.uk

it was the inevitable choice for the revived Investiture ceremony of the Prince of Wales.
Caernarfon is the home town of Bryn Terfel, a baritone of international reputation.

9.30 – 17.00

■ **Castle*** £ 4.50

Castle and town occupy what was once a short peninsula between the Rivers Seiont and Cadnant, the latter long since culverted. The castle, whose walls once rose directly from the estuary of the Seiont and which could easily

© Wales Tourist Board

> **Guided Tours** – **Guided tours** of Caernarfon and its district available from Turnstone Tours and Treks *(Waterloo Port)*.
> **Cycle Hire** – Don's Bikes (47 Pool Street); Castle Cycles (33 High Street); Cycle Hire (1 Slate Quay).
> **Beaches** – At Victoria Dock, at Port Donorwic *(east)* and at Dinas Dinlle *(southwest)*.
> **Pleasure Boat Cruises** – From Quayside, Slate Quay cruises on the Menai Strait in *Queen of the Sea* and *Snowdon Queen* – Booking Office (✆ 01286 672 772).
> **Walking** – In **South Road Park** *(A 487)*, a wooded park with lake and wildlife.

be supplied by sea, defended the southern neck of the peninsula. It had been preceded on this site by a motte-and-bailey stronghold thrown up by Hugh of Avranches, Earl of Chester, c 1090.

The castle's immense scale and unusual architectural treatment can best be appreciated from the Slate Quay to the south or from Coed Helen on the far bank of the estuary. The great citadel's silhouette is immensely enhanced by the slim turrets crowning a number of the towers, the latters' angularity emphasised by the bands of differently coloured and textured stonework. Edward's architect, almost certainly the Savoyard **James of St George**, appears to have striven to emulate the outline of the city of Constantinople, captured by Crusaders in 1204, no doubt in an attempt to express the quasi-Imperial aspirations of his master here on the shores of what has been called the "Welsh Bosphorus".

Eleven great towers and massive curtain walls protect the castle interior which is divided into two long and narrow upper and lower wards. Building started in 1283 and proceeded rapidly. In less than 10 years a complete ring of walls defending castle and town was ready, though the castle still lacked a wall and towers separating it from the town. In 1294 this allowed the rebels under Madog ap Llywelyn not only to sack the town but to take the castle as well and assassinate its sheriff. After this setback, construction proceeded apace and by 1330 was virtually complete. The castle was garrisoned until Tudor times, its design and layout being sufficiently robust to withstand the sieges of Owain Glyn Dŵr and his French allies in 1403 and 1404. Though its demolition was later ordered, its decay seems to have been slow, and was decisively brought to a halt by the restoration put in hand by its Deputy Constable, Sir Llewelyn Turner, in the last decades of the 19C.

The castle is entered through the great twin-towered **King's Gate** facing the town over Castle Ditch, which was once much wider. The gate, and the whole of this side of the castle, form part of the second, post-rebellion, phase of building (1296-1323). An array of defensive features includes a drawbridge, a series of doors and portcullises, and an inner drawbridge, as well as arrowslits and murder holes. In a canopied niche above the entrance arch is a statue of Edward II, the first "English" Prince of Wales. The inner side of the King's Gate, like a number of other features of the castle, is unfinished, a projected great hall never having been built. Beyond the remains of the Kitchens and the Well Tower is the **Eagle Tower**, the noblest of the castle's nine towers. ∎

CHIRK CASTLE ★★
(Castell Y Waun) Denbighshire

Abutting Offa's Dyke, the intimidating bulk of Chirk Castle looms above the trees of its magnificent parklands within arrow-shot of the English border marked by the River Ceiriog. It was begun in the late 13C by **Roger Mortimer**, who had been granted the lordship of Chirk by Edward I. Since 1595 it has been lived in by the Myddelton family and their descendants. A magnificent sequence of state rooms constitutes one of the finest interiors in Wales.

The castle may have been designed by the King's architect, **Master James of St George**. The original plan was for a rectangular stronghold with curtain walls incorporating half-towers, corner towers, and a south-facing gatehouse. Either the plan was not fully carried out or parts of the castle were subsequently demolished, perhaps during or after the Civil War; the towers do not extend to their full height, and the eastern and western ranges are truncated, with no corner towers. Chirk is nevertheless an awesome sight, its severity only partly relieved by the substitution of mullioned windows for arrow slits.

Michelin Atlas p 33 or Map 503 K 25

The lordship of Chirk was no guarantee of good fortune for the castle's early residents. Roger Mortimer may have held sway as Justice of Wales, but fell from favour and died in the Tower of London in 1326. At least five other owners were executed for treason while others perished on the field of battle. Repeatedly held by the Crown, Chirk was granted by Elizabeth I to her favourite, Robert Dudley, Earl of Leicester.

In 1595 it was purchased by the merchant adventurer, **Thomas Myddelton**, later Lord Mayor of London, whose family claimed descent from the fearsome Ririd Flaidd "The Wolf", a 13C lordling from far-off Merioneth. The Myddeltons and their descendants have lived here ever since, save for a lengthy interval between 1911 and 1946, when it was the home of Lord Howard de Walden, an eccentric millionaire with a passion for the Middle Ages and for the arts generally; it was he who employed Eric Gill to carve the war memorial in Chirk village. ■

COLWYN BAY

Backed by wooded hills which dip their feet in its sandy bay, this well-matured late-Victorian and Edwardian resort has little of the brashness that characterises other holiday places along the North Wales coast.

The Chester and Holyhead Railway, which reached here in 1848, was the making of Colwyn, though the resort's development really got under way only in the 1860s and 1870s.

Today's hopes are centred on the Expressway, buried in part beneath the town centre. As well as making the whole of northwest England more accessible, the new road has relieved the centre of the permanent congestion caused by through-traffic and helped the town stake its claim as an important shopping centre for the region.

(Bae Colwyn) Conwy – Population 27 002
Michelin Atlas p 33 or Map 503 I 24
Tourist Information Centres – Imperial Buildings, Station Square, Princes Drive, Colwyn Bay LL29 8LA ☎ 01492 530 478; Fax 01492 534 789.
The Promenade, Rhos-on-Sea LL28 4EP ☎ 011492 548 778.

Beaches
At Colwyn Bay and Old Colwyn *(west)*.

Promenade – The curving promenade (3mi/5km long) runs from **Rhos-on-Sea** in the west towards the village of Old Colwyn in the east. Rhos (Llandrillo-yn-Rhos) mixes red brick villas and hotels with a few older cottages to create something of the atmosphere of a fishing village. A pier once stood here, brought in bits from the Isle of Man, and now replaced by a breakwater sheltering a number of sailing dinghies.

On the promenade is the **Chapel of St Trillo**, reputedly built in the 6C over a holy well.

Welsh Mountain Zoo★ – 1mi/1.6km N by B 5113 towards Llanrwst; turn right into Old Highway. The zoo occupies an incomparable site (37 acres/15ha) high above the town among the woodlands and gardens laid out in the early 20C by the prosperous Manchester surgeon Walter Whitehead.

The zoo, founded in 1963 by the naturalist Robert Jackson, combines serious commitment to conservation and research with great popular appeal. ∎

CONWY**

Backed by the many-towered walls of its dependent town, Conwy Castle on its rocky promontory commands the Conwy estuary which for long barred the route westward into the fastness of Snowdonia. A trio of bridges, and, more recently, a boldly planned tunnel, have overcome the obstacle of the river but town and fortress still evoke the time when medieval English kings sought "to embrace and grip the intractable heart of northern Wales".

Conwy – Population 3 627
Michelin Atlas p 33 or Map 503
I 24
Tourist Information Centre
– Conwy Visitor Centre, Rosehill Street, Conwy LL32 8LD
☏ 01492 592 248, 01492 596 288.

■ Historical notes

The Cistercians were the first to settle on the west bank of the River Conwy, in 1186, though their desire to settle far from the turmoil of the world was not achieved. On several occasions during the following century, the English pursued their quarrels with the Welsh as far as Deganwy, a "crossbow-shot" away on the eastern shore, and in 1245 their soldiery pillaged the monastery. After completing his conquest of Snowdonia in 1283, Edward I determined that English control should be firmly grounded on the west bank; within days of his arrival here from Deganwy work had begun on the new stronghold and walled town, under the supervision of the Crown's great military engineer, **James of St George**. The deployment of immense resources (red sandstone from Chester to supplement the local rock, lead from Flint, iron from Staffordshire...) and the employment of a huge workforce of up to 1 500 craftsmen and labourers ensured swift completion of the great work, which was substantially ready by 1287. The monks, meanwhile, had been moved upriver to Maenan, though their place of worship remained to serve as parish church.

By the late 18C the garrison function had long since gone. Instead, Conwy had become a staging post on the way to Holyhead and Dublin, the river crossing an irritation and danger to travellers who had to brave its sometimes perilous waters and the churlishness and extortion of the ferrymen. A bridge was imperative, and was eventually – well into the 19C – provided by the genius of Thomas Telford.

Conwy Castle*** (C) – Like Caernarfon, Conwy Castle is built on a confined site which made the conventional concentric plan impossible. Instead, it is laid out in linear fashion along the narrow rocky promontory projecting into the estuary. Eight splendid drum towers stud the curtain walls, four protecting a western, **Outer Ward (C)**, four an eastern, **Inner Ward (C)** which contained the royal apartments.

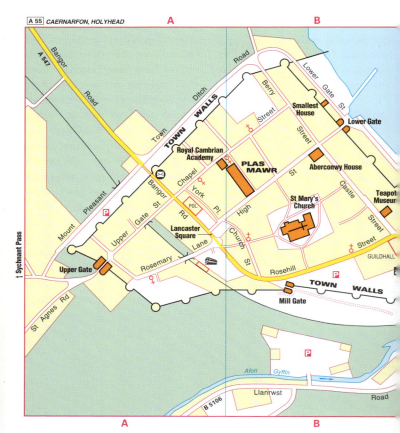

Out and About

River Trips – A trip on the *Queen Victoria*; northeast or southwest is a delightful way of enjoying the scenery of the Menai Strait, one of the most romantic waterways in Europe.

Beaches – At the Conwy Marina and Penmaenmawr *(west)*.

Today's visitors enter the castle via an excellent **visitor centre,** thence via a timber bridge and pathway. An entry once guarded by drawbridge and portcullis gives access to the **West Barbican (C)**, overlooked by two closely spaced towers.

Town Walls★★ (AB) – Edward I's bastide town is still almost wholly enclosed by the circuit of walls built in the same short period as the castle, and, like the castle, designed by **James of St George**. They are the outstanding example left in Britain of this type of urban fortification, intended to provide an advanced line of the defence of the castle as well as to protect the town itself.

Plas Mawr★★ (B) – Occupying almost the entire frontage of a narrow lane running up from the High Street, this is one of the finest town houses of the Elizabethan period in Britain. H-shaped in plan, laid out around two courtyards and with a gatehouse to the High Street frontage, Plas Mawr was built in the late 16C by Robert Wynne, a true "Elizabethan adventurer" and typical member of one of the great North Wales families who achieved wealth and prominence in Tudor times. ∎

Chapel	**C** N
East Barbican	**C** F
Inner Ward	**C** S

DENBIGH*

Overlooking the fertile Vale of Clwyd from its hilltop, this old market town is dominated by the wreck of the massive castle begun by Henry de Lacy in 1282. The natural defences of the summit (468ft/143m) may first have been strengthened by Iron Age people. Dafydd ap Gruffydd, the brother of Llywelyn ap Gruffydd, on whose death he assumed the title of Prince of Wales, held sway from here until his downfall in 1283. The lordship of Denbigh was then granted by Edward I to de Lacy, who immediately set about building his castle together with a walled town to which he granted a charter in 1290.

By the time of the 1294 uprising led by Madog ap Llywelyn, only that part of the castle's defences included in the town walls had been completed, and the Welsh were able to break in. After their ejection, the north and east walls which separate the castle from the town were built to a more rigorous specification, the effect of which can be appreciated today in the far greater thickness and bulk of construction.

Queen Elizabeth I gave the castle to her favourite, Robert Dudley,

> *(Dinbych) Denbighshire*
> *— Population 8 529*
> *Michelin Atlas p 33 or Map 503*
> *J 24*

Earl of Leicester. In 1645 the castle sheltered King Charles I, after his defeat at Rowton Moor, but the following year it was captured by Parliamentary forces and reduced to a ruin.

Denbigh Castle* – The approach to the castle leads past the site of the long-since demolished Barbican across a ditch to the **Great Gatehouse**, probably the most massive structure of its kind in Wales. Its trio of octagonal towers enclose a grand chamber, originally vaulted, but now open to the sky. High above the entrance arch is a niche containing a statue, probably of Edward I.

The grassy expanse of the castle's inner ward is still enclosed by curtain walls, though most of the buildings which were ranged inside, like the Great Hall, have been reduced to foundation level.

There are fine **views** of Denbigh in its dramatic setting, with the Vale bounded by the Clwydian Range to the east and more broken country to the west. ∎

DOLGELLAU*

On the south bank of the Wnion River, the county town of old Merionethshire has long been an important centre for the upland farming community, an important market for pedigree mountain sheep and black cattle. In the 18C-early 19C it was famous for its cottage industry of cloth-making, but the town's dominant role today is as the tourist capital of southern Snowdonia, with access down the beautiful Mawddach estuary to the coast and to the massive brooding presence of Cadair Idris just to the south.

> *Gwynedd – Population 2 632*
> *Michelin Atlas p 32-3 or Map 503 I 25*
> *Snowdonia National Park Visitor Centre – Ty Meirioin, Eldon Square, Dolgellau LL40 1PU ☎ 01341 422 888; Fax 01341 422 576.*

■ Excursions

Precipice Walk* – *3mi/5km northeast of Dolgellau by minor roads. Park in National Park car park; 3mi/5km on foot.* A favourite with Dolgellau's visitors since the estate owner laid it out in 1890, this fairly level upland walk makes an excellent introduction to the landscapes of the southern part of the National Park. The path leads at first through woodland but soon emerges on to the open land of Foel Cynwch and follows the contour round this minor massif in an anticlockwise direction. A succession of splendid panoramas opens up, from which the patronisingly worded signboards placed at intervals are unnecessary distractions. First comes Snowdonia proper, followed by the magnificent Coed y Brenin forest, the Rhinog mountains, the lovely valley of the winding Mawddach, and, finally, and gloriously, the great chair or throne of the giant Idris, Cadair Idris. The return is along the banks of Llyn Cynwch, a little lake. ■

Out and About
Walks and Rides – The Precipice Walk and the Torrent Walk have delighted visitors since the 19C; there is a more recent network of footpaths in the Coed Y Brenin Forest as well as mountain bike routes and hire *(see also below).*

ELAN VALLEY★★
(Dyffryn Elan) Powys

A century ago a series of great dams and reservoirs were built high up in mid-Wales, in the "green desert" of the Elan and Claerwen Valleys, to supply water to the growing city of Birmingham, more than 70mi to the east in the English Midlands. The fields and homesteads of a community of some 100 people, together with their church and school, vanished beneath a hundred feet of water. The design of the scheme paid great attention to its setting in these wild uplands and the catchment area has been managed with great care and sensitivity to protect wildlife and enhance the landscape. The Elan Valley has become a "Lake District" of great appeal where visitors are able to enjoy scenic drives, walking and fishing in what was one of the remotest parts of the country. The protective designation (SSSI, ESA and NNR) of much of this part of Central Wales emphasises its ecological importance and visual attractiveness.

> Michelin Atlas p 25 or Map 503 J 27
> Tourist Information Centres
> – Elan Valley Visitor Centre, Rhayader LD6 5HP
> ☎ 01597 810 898.
> The Leisure Centre, North Street, Rhayader LD6 5BU ☎ 01597 810 591.

■ **Historical notes**

Towards the end of the 19C Birmingham City Council, under the leadership of Joseph Chamberlain, was urgently looking for abundant and reliable sources of fresh water for its expanding industries and close-packed population; the ravages of cholera spread by polluted water supplies earlier in the century had not been forgotten. The Elan area, with its high rainfall, suitably shaped valleys, and impermeable rocks was ideally suited.

Work began on the immense project in 1893. A total of 50 000 navvies were employed, labouring in what for the time were excellent conditions of work; to ensure this, as well as to maintain strict control of the quality of work, Birmingham Corporation preferred to carry out the scheme itself rather than put it in the hands of contractors. A superb example of municipal confidence and enterprise, the Birmingham Water Supply Scheme was opened with great pomp in the presence of King Edward VII, Queen Alexandra, and the Lord Mayor.

This was the first phase of the project, consisting of the three dams on the Elan and the base of one of the three planned dams on the Claerwen. When the time came to implement this second phase, advances in technology made it possible for a single dam to perform the work of the projected three. The Claerwen Dam, the largest in the scheme, was completed in 1952. The dams are best seen with water cascading over them, but the Elan Valley is popular at most times of the year and can become congested at times.

Visitor Centre – The Centre is housed in the original main construction workshop close to the foot of the Caban Coch dam. Its varied displays, including audio-visual programmes, give an account not only of the construction, royal opening and operation of the scheme but also of the history and ecology of the area, marking the contrast in flora and fauna between meadow and woodland and the calm waters of the reservoirs and the fast-flowing mountain streams. There are reminders that Shelley passed some time in the now-submerged country houses of Cwm Elan and Nant Gwyllt, denouncing the poverty and injustice of the social conditions of rural Wales but also penning the lines:

"Woods, to whose depths
returns to die
The wounded echo's melody".

The Elan curves past the meadow where the Centre is sited, below the windows of the restaurant, and flows beneath a charming small suspension bridge, now superseded by a stark modern structure giving access to **Elan Village**. This, the successor to the hutments which housed the construction force, has garden city-type cottages and a handsome school, now an outdoor pursuits centre.

Caban Coch Dam and Reservoir* – The dam, its colossal scale (122ft/37m high and 610ft/186m long) emphasised by rustic masonry and giant-sized coping stones, makes an excellent introduction to the fine engineering works of the scheme as a whole.

Water released from this reservoir (capacity 7 187 million gallons/ 35 530 megalitres) maintains the flow of the Elan and thence of the

---

Craft Centres – For pottery visit **Marston Pottery** (*Lower Cefn Faes, Rhayader*) and for glassware visit **Welsh Royal Crystal** (*see below*).
Wildlife Centres – Some nature reserves provide the opportunity to see the **red kite**, other birds of prey and other wildlife - **Gilfach Farm Longhouse** (*4mi/6km north of Rhayader by A 470 and a minor road east*); **Gigrin Farm** (*0.5mi/0.8km south of Rhayader by A 470 and a minor road east*).

Wye, source of much of the water supply of southeast Wales.

Garreg-ddu Dam★ – *1mi/1.5km upstream.* As Caban Coch is at too low a level for water to run by gravity alone as far as Birmingham, the Garreg-ddu dam impounds water which is taken off at the Foel Tower, a fine example of what has been styled "Birmingham Baroque". From here the water flows along an aqueduct (73mi/117km long) at 2mph/3kph down an apparently shallow gradient (1 in 2 200), which is steep enough to obviate the need for pumping. The dam also serves as a viaduct giving access to the Claerwen Valley.

Dol-y-Mynach and Claerwen Dam and Reservoir★★ – *4.5mi/ 7km west of Garreg-ddu.* The road up to the Claerwen dam passes through fine woods of oak, beech and larch, crossing the occasional torrent rushing to the river below. There is a glimpse of the majestic foundations of the never-completed Dol-y-Mynach dam. The boggy terrain upstream is a haven for bird life, which can be observed from a hide. ■

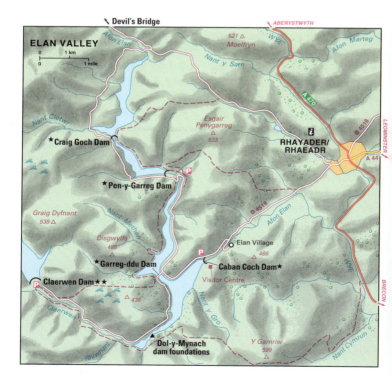

ERDDIG ★★

Wrexham

Michelin Atlas p 33/34 or Map 503 K 24

Among the most appealing of the National Trust's country houses, Erddig has a fascination due less to its architecture than to the way it evokes the three centuries of life led in it, not only by its masters but by its entire population of servants, skivvies, estate workers and ladies' companions.

■ Historical notes

Erddig's first owner and builder was Joshua Edisbury, High Sheriff of Denbighshire, who completed his country residence here on the outskirts of then fashionable Wrexham in the 1680s. The expense bankrupted him; John Meller, the lawyer involved in his bankruptcy proceedings, was the next owner, but in 1733 the estate became the property of the **Yorke** family, in whose hands it remained until 1973.

The Yorkes, invariably named Simon or Philip, seem to have been engaging, mildly eccentric, and to have enjoyed an unusually intimate relationship with those that served them. Nothing was ever thrown away, unusually complete records and accounts were kept, and servants were treated as individuals, more portraits being painted (and later, photographs taken) of them than of the family, and their characteristics and achievements celebrated in whimsical verse. The epitaph of Simon I (d 1767) reads *"a very mild, just and benevolent character... An advantage which Amiable Men have over great Ones"*, while Philip I, an antiquarian and scholar, was referred to by the sporting writer Nimrod as *"the worst horseman I ever saw in the saddle"*.

By the mid 20C Erddig was in trouble; the family's fortune was depleted and the house was being steadily attacked by subsidence from coalmining. The last Simon sat helplessly in Wellington boots surrounded by buckets and chamber pots to catch the water streaming in through the ruined roof. After his death in 1966, it seemed that demolition was Erddig's inevitable fate. His successor, the last Philip, struggled valiantly for a few more years, then gave house and grounds to the National Trust. After the biggest rescue operation ever undertaken by the Trust, Erddig was opened to the public in 1977.

■ Tour

Outbuildings – Erddig is entered not through the main door but via the extensive outbuildings, "offices" and servants' quarters, which give an excellent idea of the complexity of the domestic economy which sustained the life of a squire's family.

The route from the **Estate Yard** (still in use as the house's maintenance depot) to the Kitchen passes the **Kennel Yard** where the hounds were kept and fed from their own kitchen, the **Lime Yard** and **Saw Mill** (short video film on Erddig's restoration), the coarsely-cobbled **Midden yard**, the **Stable Yard** with the family vehicles, the **Brewhouse**, **Bakehouse** and **Laundry Yard** with its hanging linen.

Servants' Quarters – Hare and pheasant lend an authentic atmosphere to the **Kitchen**, where the main meals were prepared, lesser meals like breakfast and tea being prepared in the **Still Room**. The passageway is lined with servants' photographs with captions in verse.

Agent's Office and **Housekeeper's Room** were the abode of Mr Hughes and Mrs Brown respectively, the last to preside over Erddig's affairs in the early 20C before decline set in. The **Servants' Hall** shows the extent of the Yorkes' interest in those that looked after them; there are two sets of **servants' portraits** with doggerel verses, the first from the 1790s, the second from the 1830s, with bold representations of carpenters, a woodman, a gamekeeper, kitchen man and housemaid, even of a Black coachboy (early 18C). Two long-serving butlers were honoured with hatchment memorials.

Interior – Throughout the Yorkes' occupation, Erddig remained mostly furnished with the pieces the family had brought with them in the early 18C. Nor were any significant alterations carried out after John Meller had extended the house by adding wings to the original building. This makes Erddig's rooms almost uncannily evocative; as well as be-

© Wales Tourist Board

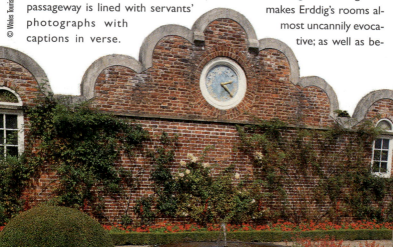

ing *"a treasure house of 18C furniture, porcelain and glass"* (W Condry), it feels as if a member of the Yorke family might appear at any moment, particularly since the National Trust has made every effort to present many of the rooms as they would have been used by the Yorkes at the end of the 19C.

Thus the **Dining Room** with its array of family portraits, has its table laid in accordance with Mrs Beeton's 1901 edition of Household Management, and Louisa Yorke's records of meals eaten and entertainments provided can be seen. The **Saloon** has a metal ceiling; the Yorkes feared fire, and this is one of a number of fire-resistant measures introduced throughout the house. The symmetry of the garden layout can be appreciated from the windows. The **Tapestry Room** has early-18C Soho tapestries, the adjoining **Chinese Room** 18C Chinese painted wallpaper. The **Library** is as it was when used by Philip Yorke II c 1910; the little 17C portraits were drawn to illustrate his ancestor, Philip I's history of the Royal Tribes of Wales published in 1799. As the west-facing Entrance Hall proved draughty in use, the main entrance was moved to the lower ground floor and the hall turned into a **Music Room**; the instruments on display include a 19C Gothick organ. The **Drawing Room** was where the last of the Yorkes, Philip III, made his final stand. Late into the 20C Erddig had no mains water, no gas or electricity; a photograph here shows him reading by a bottled gas flame, whose feeble light was somewhat magnified by an arrangement of reflectors made from 18C silver salvers. In the **Red Bedroom**, the coat of arms was made in cut paperwork by Betty Ratcliffe, for many years the companion of Simon I's widow. Less favoured maids lived in the **Attic Bedrooms**.

The dark-panelled **Long Gallery** is a survival from Erddig's earliest days. The **State Bedroom** has an Oriental flavour; its centrepiece is the State Bed of 1720, which has miraculously recovered from its periodic soaking by rainwater.

Attendance at the **Chapel** was compulsory well into the 20C, the family entering from the Chinese Room, the servants through another door. On the lower ground floor, the **Tribes Room** serves as a **family museum**, the most poignant items being those recalling the varied life of the last Philip, actor with the Arthur Brough players of Folkestone, keen cyclist, Education Corps sergeant in the Second World War, and travel courier on cultural holidays to Spain.

Gardens** – Together with Powis Castle, Erddig's gardens bear rare witness to the formal style of landscaping all but swept away in the course of the 18C pursuit of naturalness and informality. ■

HARLECH CASTLE★★
Gwynedd

Standing four-square on its rock against a spectacular background of sea and mountain, Harlech Castle has inevitably become the very image of a medieval stronghold, its strength the inspiration for the song *Men of Harlech*. The little town of Harlech lies on the southwest border of the Snowdonia National Park and it is a good base from which to explore the mountains inland.

■ Historical notes
In layout similar to Beaumaris, Harlech Castle was one of the "Iron Ring" of fortresses rapidly run up by Edward I to secure his conquest of North Wales. Although its crag overlooking the sea seems a natural site for a stronghold, there is no trace of any earlier fortification, despite a reference to a court at "Harddllech" in the story of Princess Branwen in

Michelin Atlas p 32 or Map 503 H 25
Snowdonia National Park Visitor Centre – Gwyddfor House, High Street,
Harlech LL46 2YA ☏ 01766 780 658; Fax 01766 780 658.

> **Beaches**
> At Harlech, Llandanwg and Dyffryn Ardudwy.

the *Mabinogion*. The builder of the castle was the redoubtable **Master James of St George**, Edward's Savoyard architect, who resided here as Constable between 1290 and 1293. In anticipation of attack from landward, the castle was built to be supplied by sea (which reached to the foot of the crag until the 18C) via a watergate. This enabled it to withstand the besieging forces of Madog ap Llywelyn during the revolt of 1294-95, though it fell to Owain Glyn Dŵr in 1404 and briefly became his seat of power before being retaken in 1408 by the future Henry V. The castle demonstrated its importance and the quality of its defences on two more occasions, being the last Lancastrian and the last Royalist stronghold to fall in the Wars of the Roses and the Civil War respectively.

■ Tour

With its high walls and sextet of massive outward-facing drum towers, the castle completely dominates the small town of sloping streets gathered around it. Defended more than adequately by cliffs and crags, it was only on the eastern side that it was vulnerable to attack and it is here that the most elaborate fortifications were built. The splendid **gatehouse** is approached across a ditch cut in the rock, originally via a bridge with two towers. An outer gate with twin turrets elegantly corbelled out stands in the outer curtain wall, much of which is in ruins. Beyond the constricted outer ward are the awesome outer towers of the gatehouse and a whole series of obstacles including three doors and portcullises. The gatehouse contained comfortable suites of rooms for the Constable, his high status expressed by the sophisticated architectural treatment of the **courtyard façade,** with its elegant corner turrets and six great windows. The inner ward is made to seem smaller by the scale of its walls; from the sentry-walk there are stupendous **views** over the coastal levels of Morfa Harlech and north to Snowdonia.

Outside the castle, a striking modern (1984) equestrian statue takes as its theme a tragic episode from the *Mabinogion* in which the British king Bendigeidfran lost his nephew Gwern in battle. ■

HOLYHEAD

Reached by the great causeway which Thomas Telford built in 1822 to link Anglesey to Holy Island, Holyhead has long been the main port connecting England and Wales with Ireland, particularly with the capital, Dublin.

(Caergybi) Anglesey – Population 12 569
Michelin Atlas p 32 or Map 503 G 24
Tourist Information Centre – Penrhos Beach Road, Holyhead LL65 2QB
☏ 01407 762 622.

■ Historical notes

Holyhead harbour is essentially a 19C creation but the port's maritime history goes back to the Roman naval base founded here in the late 3C AD in an attempt to control pirates in the Irish Sea; its walls still stand, forming an enclosure around the parish church, which is dedicated to St Cybi, the Celtic saint who settled here in the 6C. The town's Welsh name, Caergybi – Cybi's Fort – reflects these beginnings.

By the early 17C packet boats were operating on a regular basis between Holyhead and Dublin, despite the need for travellers to cross both the Menai Strait and the channel separating Holy Island from the rest of Anglesey. By the late 18C traffic had increased dramatically. The construction of Telford's **Holyhead Road** (now A 5) and the Menai Bridge went in parallel with the improvement of the **Inner Harbour**, completed in 1821. Steam packets had been introduced in 1817 and the first steam locomotive pulled its boat train into the harbour station in 1850. Between 1845 and 1873 an army of workmen toiled to build the great **breakwater** (nearly 2mi/3km long) to protect the calm water of the **New Harbour**, one of Britain's official ports of refuge, a haven where vessels could ride out the fiercest storms.

The completion of the North Wales Expressway (A 55) has encouraged road traffic at the expense of rail, and Irish Sea traffic now mostly consists of cars and trucks using the roll-on roll-off ferries.

Few visitors break their journey here, except when the ferries are stopped by bad weather, but the busy town has something of the allure of all ports. It is also a base for exploring the magnificent coast of Holy Island which curls around the base of Holyhead Mountain.

Schools and the Welsh language

Education in the 18C and the 19C was largely in the hands of the Nonconformist churches. In 1846 three English lawyers were sent as part of a government commission to assess Welsh schools. Their report, known in Wales as "The Treason of the Blue Books", attacked Welsh as a language of slavery and ignorance, and condemned its use by pupils and teachers. Even among the Welsh themselves, use of the language was regarded as a social and economic obstacle, and determined efforts were made to stamp it out. This campaign culminated in the notorious Welsh Not, a system of punishment whereby children caught speaking Welsh were obliged to wear around the neck a wooden board, on which the words "Welsh Not" were painted. By 1901 the policy had taken its toll and only 50% of the population still spoke the Welsh language.

■ Sights

Harbour – The Inner Harbour and the railway station stand in cosy proximity to the town centre, strung out along the low protective hill immediately to the west. The station approach has a fine cast-iron clock commemorating the visit of the Prince of Wales in 1880. Another royal visit, albeit an involuntary one, is marked by the Doric **Admiralty Arch** (1821), which marks this end of the London-Holyhead Road as the southern end in the capital city is marked by the Marble Arch; it honours George IV, delayed here for several days by a storm in 1821 until persuaded to venture aboard a newfangled steamboat. The great expanse of water sheltered by the breakwater can be appreciated from Beach Road and the Lower Promenade.

The **Maritime Museum** is housed in what is believed to be the oldest surviving Lifeboat House (1858) in Wales. ■

Out and About

Beaches – At Porth Dafarch, Trearddur Bay and Borth Wen.

Boat Trips – Holyhead is only a short sea crossing away from the *craic* and Guinness and Georgian architecture of Dublin.

Craftwork – High above the town centre is the **Ucheldre Centre**, a former convent chapel which has been tastefully converted into an arts and exhibition centre, often with displays of local interest.

KNIGHTON*

This small town on the Herefordshire border began as a Saxon settlement on an easily defended knoll overlooking the River Teme. The natural defensive qualities of the site were reinforced by the alignment along its western end of the great earthwork known as Offa's Dyke. Around 1100 the Normans built their first castle mound, Bryn-y-Castell, in the valley below but about 80 years later moved their fortress to the strongpoint on the knoll. Knighton serves as a market centre for the Teme valley and, being roughly halfway along the long-distance footpath following **Offa's Dyke**, makes a good base for exploring this part of the border country.

(Tref-y-Clawdd) Powys
– Population 2 851
Michelin Atlas p 25 or Map 503 K 26
Tourist Information Centre
– Offa's Dyke Centre, West Street, Knighton LD7 1EN ☏ 01547 529 424 (see below).

■ Sights

Offa's Dyke Centre – Housed in a 19C school building, the Centre has displays on the history of the Dyke and on its use today. The **long-distance footpath** (177mi/285km) which largely follows the course of Offa's Dyke was painstakingly stitched together over a long period and was officially opened in 1971. It passes through some of the most splendid scenery of the borderlands between England and Wales.

A border barrier from sea to sea – *"Rex nomine Offa qui vallum magnum inter Britanniam atque Merciam de mare usque ad mare facere imperavit"* wrote Bishop Asser in the late 9C, a century after the Mercian king's reign. His statement, that "a king named Offa... commanded a great bank to be built between the land of the Britons – ie the Welsh – and Mercia all the way from sea to sea", provides the only evidence we have that it was indeed Offa, ruler of Mercia throughout the second half of the 8C AD, who gave orders for the construction of the earthwork that stretches – not without interruption – from the Severn Estuary to the coast of North Wales.

The Dyke is one of the most impressive monuments in Britain, even in its present eroded state. Originally it may have stood higher (as much as 40ft/12m), with a ditch normally on the western side. That it marked the boundary between Offa's powerful Saxon kingdom and the domains of the Welsh princelings seems clear but whether it was primarily a defensive barrier or simply a demarcation line remains unclear. Its alignment also presents puzzles; parts of it were obviously surveyed in masterly fashion, running from one viewpoint to another. A zigzag course may have resulted from sightlines being obscured by woodland. In places the Dyke is absent altogether; was this because there were no territorial disputes with the local Welsh, or as a result of natural barriers like floodlands and forests being adequate?

■ Excursions

Offa's Dyke★ — *9.5mi/15.5km northwest of Knighton; leaflet available at Offa's Dyke Centre.*

The uplands of Clun Forest (just in England) have one of the most spectacular sections of the Dyke. The stretch between Springhill Farm and **Llanfair Hill** has been described as "perhaps the most magnificent of all" (CJ Wright). To the southeast the great earthwork can be followed across the moorlands to its highest point (1 408ft/427m).

Powys County Observatory — *2.5mi/4km southeast of Knighton by A 4113, a minor road and rough track.* This recently constructed small observatory high up in the hills between Knighton and Presteigne has a *camera obscura* and a planetarium as well as a 13in/34cm refracting telescope. There is also a meteorological station which images views of the earth's weather from satellite. ■

© Wales Tourist Board

LLANBERIS★

The starting point for the easiest ascent of Snowdon on foot or by rail, this mountain village has a number of other attractions which make it one of the most popular centres in Snowdonia.

The original settlement was at the hamlet of Nant Peris, at the entrance to the awesome **Pass of Llanberis,** but the modern village has grown up on the southwestern shore of Llyn Padarn, a fine stretch of water separated from an upper lake, Llyn Peris, by a narrow isthmus. Copper was extracted in the area at the end of the 18C but Llanberis owes fame and fortune to the immense quantities of slate quarried from the Cambrian rock which makes up the great mass of Elidir Fach (2 565ft/782m) rising from the lakeside.

Welsh Slate Museum★ – Two centuries of quarrying have carved the slaty southwestern flanks of Elidir Fach into a series of gigantic steps which seem to

> Gwynedd – Population 1 986
> Michelin Atlas p 32 or Map 503 H 24
> Local map p 98
> Tourist Information Centre – 41a High Street, Llanberis LL55 4EU
> ☎ 01286 870 765; Fax 01286 871 951; llanberis.tic@gwynedd.gov.uk

lead to the very summit of the mountain.

At the foot of the reshaped mountain a handsome range of buildings with corner towers, clock tower and entrance arch is laid out around a courtyard. Here were the repair workshops of the great **Dinorwig Quarry**, whose skilled workforce could make and maintain anything from a cogwheel to a locomotive. The workshops were in daily use until the quarry closed in 1969; they now house the Welsh Slate Museum, a branch of the National Museum. This is a living museum with a completely authentic atmosphere, which not only tells the history of this important industry but also carries out repair work for other branches of the museum.

Padarn Country Park – The park is laid out along the banks of Llyn Padarn and on the lower oak-clad slopes of Elidir Fach, sharing ap-

> **Craft Centre**
> Unique slate, wrought-iron and wooden products are available in the gift shop at the **Welsh Slate Museum** (see below).

proach road and car park with the Slate Museum and Llanberis Lake Railway. The Vivian Quarry, part of the Dinorwig enterprise, reaches some 450ft/135m up the mountain and down into a 50ft/15m pit, now flooded. Slate extraction was always a perilous operation. Men worked long hours high up on the exposed mountainside, liable to falls and to slips on greasy wet slate, to injuries caused by sharp fragments and to crushing by machinery. The old **Quarry Hospital**, now the **Visitor Centre**, details these conditions, and also has displays on the local environment.

Llanberis Lake Railway – The problems of transporting heavy loads of slate to the coast in the early days of quarrying was only partly solved by the use of sleds, boats on Llyn Padarn and packhorses. In 1824 a horse tramway was built, succeeded in 1849 by a steam railway which brought the slate down to purpose-built Port Dinorwic (Y Felinheli) on the Menai Strait. The railway closed in 1961 but its lakeside trackbed has been relaid with narrow-gauge rails along which the little engines which once worked in the quarries pull impressively-long tourist trains.

Snowdon Mountain Railway★★ – Llanberis is the base station for the narrow-gauge rack-and-pinion railway completed in 1896 to haul passengers to the summit of Snowdon. The only railway of its type in Britain, it is operated by a fleet of sturdy little steam engines based on the prototypes built by the Locomotiv-und Maschinenfabrik of Winterthur in Switzerland, though more recently motive power has also been supplied by diesel locomotives and railcars. By 1995, No 2, *Enid,* built in 1895, had travelled almost a quarter of a million miles (c 400 000km).

The only level section of track is in Llanberis station, where workshops and coaling facilities lend all the atmosphere of a Victorian railway; the rest of the run (4.5mi/7km) is at an average gradient of 1 in 7.8 with a maximum gradient of 1 in 5.5. The locomotives propel the single carriages of each train from the rear, past woodlands and waterfalls initially, then through open sheep country dotted with abandoned farm buildings. A pause is made at Halfway Station to take on water and allow a descending train to pass. Given clear weather, the mountain views become ever more spectacular as the train chugs higher, past Clogwyn Station to arrive at Summit Station (3 493ft/1 065m above sea level). After enjoying the incomparable **panorama**★★★ from the summit cairn, passengers can fortify themselves for the descent in the café, the successor to a hotel which itself had been preceded by mountain huts first erected in the 1840s. ■

LLANDUDNO*

Llandudno is one of the finest examples of a planned seaside resort in Great Britain, with its broad promenade and stuccoed hotels laid out on the isthmus linking the limestone headlands of the Great Orme and the Little Orme. The town owes its elegant appearance to the careful planning undertaken by the local landowners, the prominent Mostyn family, and their architect, Owen Williams. Llandudno is also an excellent urban base for exploring both the North Wales coast and Snowdonia.

> Conwy – Population 18 647
> Michelin Atlas p 33 or Map 503 I 24
> Tourist Information Centre – 1-2
> Chapel Street, Llandudno LL30 2YU
> ☎ 01492 876 413; Fax 01492 872 722.

■ Historical notes

Until the middle years of the 19C, there was little more to Llandudno than a few copper miners' cottages clinging to the slopes of the Great Orme and the occasional fisherman's shack dotted about on the sandy wasteland facing the curving shoreline.

Aware both of the need to solve his family's pressing financial problems and of the potential of the sandy wasteland for development as a resort, the Hon E M L Mostyn is supposed to have commissioned Williams to prepare a feasibility study while the pair were sheltering from a sudden downpour in a bathing hut. An early proposal would have made Llandudno the packet station for Ireland, short-circuiting Holyhead. This came to nothing but an Act of Parliament of 1854 gave the Mostyns strict control over the form development should take, allowing them to set the high architectural and social

© Wales Tourist Board

> **Out and About**
> **Bus Tour** – The **Guide Friday Bus Tour** takes in the town centre of Llandudno and Conwy.
> **Craft Centres** – The craft shop in the **Oriel Mostyn Art Gallery** *(see below)*, approved by the Crafts Council, offers jewellery, ceramics, glassware and hand-woven textiles.
> **Entertainment** – The **Aberconwy Centre (BY)** for sports and entertainment and the **North Wales Theatre** (1 500-seats) *(at the western end of the seafront)*.
> **Beaches** – On the North Shore (dogs permitted).

tone which Llandudno has striven to maintain ever since. Commerce was kept away from the seafront, building heights and road widths were carefully specified, as were the dimensions of rooms and windows. No cellar was to be converted into a separate dwelling. Williams created the sweeping crescent of the Promenade, and *St George's Hotel* (1854) was soon joined by others to form a continuous line along the seafront. The streets behind were laid out in a grid pattern which guided the town's development until it reached the West Shore (1mi/1.5km away).

Llandudno's heyday came at the end of the 19C, when its population trebled and quadrupled during the summer season and it succeeded in squaring the circle of popularity and exclusivity; expensive shops in canopied Mostyn Street served the clientele of the grand hotels and entertainment was provided by Prof Beaumont, the Escapologist, and by Signor Ferraria and his Performing Birds.

■ Seafront★ (BY)

Owen Williams had no regrets about the generous dimensions of his promenade, and claimed he would have made it even wider had resources permitted. It is anchored firmly to the foot of the Great Orme by the seven-storey bulk of the *Grand Hotel*, breasting the waves like a man-made extension of the headland itself, and by the **Pier★ (BX)**. The Pavilion, which once seated an audience of 2 000, was destroyed by fire but the Pier (1 400ft/427m) still protrudes into the sea. It dates from 1875 and was once compared to "a maharajah's palace floating in a lake"; its kiosks, ironwork and end pavilion are a delicious confection of exotic, Indo-Gothick detailing. In contrast to many other piers, but like the town itself, it is in good shape, and a stroll along its great length is a cheerful experience, not least for the view of the Promenade in its entirety. The continuous line of pale stucco hotels, uniquely in Britain, has been preserved intact. Referred to wryly by Clough Williams-Ellis as "Pimlico Palladian", the architecture was already old-fashioned at the time of building. There are few highlights, rather an impression of restraint and good manners. The greatest variety is seen at the end nearest the pier, where the land rises and a few surviving elm trees separate Promenade and hotels, creating an almost Mediterranean ambience.

Visitors are sometimes surprised to see Llandudno's lifeboat passing through the streets; the lifeboat station is in Lloyd Street, enabling the vessel to be towed rapidly to the north or the west shore.

Alice in Wonderland Centre (BY) – *Trinity Square*. Animated tableaux celebrate the adventures of *Alice in Wonderland* and *Through the Looking Glass*, inspired by the

> **Access**
> There is a steep and narrow road to the top for cars and several footpaths for pedestrians.
> The **Great Orme Tramway★ (AX)**, completed in 1903, gives an exhilarating ride in vintage, cable-hauled tramcars from the west end of the town up to the terminus on the summit.
> The **Llandudno Cable-car (AX)** is a more modern alternative, starting from the west end of the seafront.

fact the Alice Liddell and her family took their holidays in Llandudno.

■ The Great Orme★

Victorian Llandudno was fortunate in having its own mountain (679ft/207m) rising ruggedly from the very seashore. The limestone headland, a prominent landmark visible along much of the North Wales coast, is a strange mixture of wild nature, long human history, and visitor amenities. ■

Augusta St.	BY	2
Chapel St.	AY	3
Clarence Crescent	BY	4
Deganwy Ave.	AY	5
Gloddaeth St	AY	6
Madoc St	AY	7
Maelgwyn Rd	AY	9
Mostyn Ave.	BY	12
Mostyn Broadway	BY	13
Mostyn Champneys Retail Park	BY	
Mostyn St.	BY	14
North Parade	ABX	16
Oxford Rd	BY	18
St Mary's Rd.	AY	20
Trinity St.	BY	22
Tudor Crescent	BY	24
Upper Mostyn St.	AY	25
Vaughan St	BY	26
Victoria Centre	BY	

Oriel Mostyn Art Gallery ...... BY K

LLANGOLLEN*

Of several river valleys penetrating from the English lowlands deep into the mountains of North Wales, the **Vale of Llangollen*** has long been considered the most picturesque. The little market town and resort of Llangollen is popular with visitors throughout the year but is best known for its International Musical *Eisteddfod,* held in July, when singers and dancers from dozens of countries fill its streets and perform to packed audiences in the striking new Royal International Pavilion.

A gateway into Wales – Before breaking out eastward into the English plain, the winding River Dee follows geological fault-lines between the slaty Berwyn Mountains to the south and the

> Denbighshire – Population 3 267
> Michelin Atlas p 33 or Map 503 K 25
> Tourist Information Centre – Town Hall, Castle Street, Llangollen LL20 5PD
> ☎ 01978 860 828; Fax 01978 861 563.

magnificent limestone scarp of the Eglwyseg Mountain to the north. The contrast between these stark uplands and the homely, intimate vale with its lush woodlands and verdant pastures seems almost to have been designed with the sensibilities of late-18C and early-19C travellers in mind; in 1798, on his 20th birthday, Hazlitt chose "this enchanted spot" to read from Rousseau's *Nouvelle Héloise,* and Paul Sandby paused at Llangollen on his extended sketching

tour of the North in 1771. Later visitors included Southey, Shelley, Wordsworth and Sir Walter Scott, as well as figures like the Duke of Wellington and his friend Prince Paul Eszterhazy, all of whom were received by the eccentric pair known as the "Ladies of Llangollen" *(see p 83)*.

By the time of Hazlitt's musings, the great engineer Thomas Telford had begun work on the ambitious canal project linking the Mersey, Dee and Severn; a spur to Llangollen was built, as well as two of the finest monuments of the Canal Age, the great aqueducts at Pont Cysyllte and Chirk. Years later, in 1815, Telford returned to the area to build what is still admired as a superb example of highway engineering, the great turnpike road across the mountains linking London to Holyhead and thence to Ireland, newly joined to Britain by the Act of Union of 1800. Finally the railway arrived in 1862, eventually linking the industrial cities of Northern England with Bala, Dolgellau and the shores of Cardigan Bay, and bringing different kinds and increased numbers of tourists to Llangollen itself.

Llangollen Bridge – Two centuries ago, Llangollen consisted of straggling Bridge Street to the south and a village green to the north, linked by the bridge known as one of the "Seven Wonders of Wales". Given an extra span to accommodate the railway in 1873 and carefully widened in 1969, the four-arched bridge probably dates from c 1500 but was preceded by an earlier structure supposedly built by the Bishop of St Asaph in the mid 14C. The Dee here has the character of a wild river, crashing and foaming over rocky outcrops where willow trees somehow maintain a precarious hold. The bridge acts as an informal grandstand for spectators enthralled by the numerous national and international canoe and slalom festivals held every year. To the north, the land rises steeply to the canal, while to the south, the town's main

---

Out and About

Craft Centre – Y Glassblobbery *(15mi/24km west by A 5 and A 494)* offers hand-made ornamental glassware; also ccontemporary and traditional craftwork. At the **Craft Workshop** *(Berwyn lodge, Glynbdyfrdwy; 5mi/8km west of Llangollen)* the building is decorated with the product – large decorative butterflies.

Dee Valley – The delightful scenery of the river valley may be explored with the minimum of energy and stress by railway upstream or by canal downstream *(see below)*.

shopping street, Castle Street, is part of a modest mid-19C town planning scheme which directed Llangollen's growth into a grid pattern of streets to the west.

Llangollen Railway* – *North bank.* There is only just room for the curving tracks and platforms of Llangollen Station between the Dee and the steep slope to the north. The whistling and hooting of steam and diesel locomotives heard over the roar of the river contribute to the authentic atmosphere of a mid-20C railway, recreated by the enthusiasts who have reopened several miles of the old Ruabon-Barmouth line shut in the 1960s. The regular services, run on what is the only standard-gauge preserved railway in Wales, are perhaps the best way of exploring

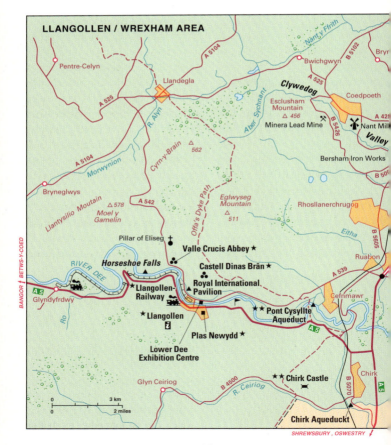

the Vale upstream from Llangollen as far as Glyndyfrdwy; continuation to Corwen is planned.

Llangollen Wharf — *North bank.* The Llangollen branch of the Shropshire Union Canal was built by Telford mainly as a feeder supplying water to the system from the River Dee but it was used for commercial traffic too. The horse-drawn passenger service initiated in 1884 has been revived, and a leisurely barge trip on the winding waterway along the lower slopes of the Vale is a most relaxing way of enjoying the varied scenery downstream from Llangollen. Upstream, the towpath follows the narrowing canal to join the Dee at Telford's **Horseshoe Falls**, a curving weir of great elegance in a romantic setting.

Victorian School and Museum — *Parade Street.* A loving re-creation of the severe atmosphere of a late-19C schoolroom occupies, appropriately enough, a Victorian school building of 1868. Here groups of today's children may don Victorian clothes and sit at desks with inkwells, writing on slates with squeaky chalk, studying maps of the British Empire, and obeying the blackboard's admonition to be "seen and not heard". Other rooms evoke local history and Victorian domestic life.

Royal International Pavilion — *Northwest of town centre by A 542.* The fabric of its canopy gleaming white against the lush green western outskirts of Llangollen, this extraordinary structure was opened in 1992 primarily to house the events of the International Eisteddfod. Its tensioned PVC-coated polyester is hung from a steel arch (75ft/23m high with a span of 196ft/60m), covering a permanent arena (2 000 seats) which can be extended to shelter

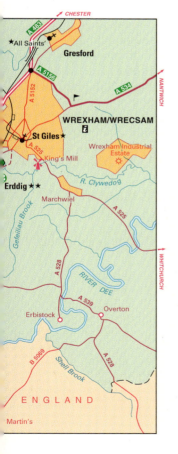

an audience of a further 3 000. The monster marquee, a triumph of innovative technology, merges with more conventional structures housing more cultural and leisure facilities — exhibitions, concerts, films shows and conferences.

"Blessed is a World that sings, Gentle are its songs". The motto of the **International Musical Eisteddfod** was coined in 1947, when the festival made its first attempt to link the world with music and friendship, and singers and dancers representing 14 nations found their way to Llangollen. Since then the annual festival, held in July, has welcomed performers from virtually every country in the world. Among them, as a young man, was Luciano Pavarotti but stars are the exception; most performers remain anonymous members of choirs and folklore troupes, whose bright costumes make a welcome splash of colour in the local townscape. Each July, some 12 000 participants from up to 50 countries make their way here and are somehow found a place in the hotels and private houses of the town and its surroundings, while their performances are watched by crowds totalling 120 000, making this one of the most important events of its kind in the world.

Castell Dinas Brân* — *Steep way-marked footpath north of Llangollen.* The stronghold built by a local lord in the mid 13C seems to have had a useful life of only a few years before being burnt down in the course of the First Welsh War of 1277. Its new Anglo-Norman owner found the banks of the Dee at Holt

Eisteddfod

The **International Musical Eisteddfod**, held annually in Llangollen, is attended by dancers, singers and players from more than 50 countries (early July); it celebrated its 50th anniversary in 1996. A **National Eisteddfod** has been held every year, alternating between north and south Wales, since 1858 when thousands attended the festival held that year in Llangollen. An **eisteddfod** (plural **eisteddfodau**) is a Welsh language cultural festival, inspired by a competition between bards held in 1789 in Corwen in the Owain Glyndŵr tavern and based on the strong musical tradition which finds expression in the many local choirs; there is one in almost every village and town and many admit visitors to listen to their rehearsals.

more congenial, and erected his castle there rather than taking up residence on this exposed hilltop some 750ft/c 240m above Llangollen. Since then the rectangular castle, built within the earthen ramparts of an Iron-Age fortification, has slowly crumbled away, ignored until the late 18C, when its craggy outline was seen to fulfil all the requirements of a Romantic ruin and it became the most famous landmark in the Vale of Llangollen.

■ Excursions

Llangollen Motor Museum – *1mi/km by A 539*. Two forms of transport are combined here in an exhibition which tells the story of British canals and the people who worked on them, while the veteran cars evoke the early days of motoring.

Pont Cysyllte Aqueduct** – *4mi/7km east of Llangollen by A 539*. The official portrait of **Thomas Telford** poses him against the background of this splendid aqueduct which carries the Ellesmere Canal 121ft/37m above the River Dee. The expression on the face of the great engineer is one of confidence and satisfaction, and Pont Cysyllte, built 1795-1810, was indeed a remarkably original achievement. Telford rejected the conventional solution to the problem of crossing a deep valley, a series of locks and a short bridge, in favour of a structure springing directly from the valley's northern rim to the tip of a huge embankment on the far side. The canal, together with its towpath, is carried in a cast-iron trough (1007ft/307m long), supported on four iron arches resting on 18 elegantly tapering stone piers, the upper parts of which are hollow. Alternative recipes are given for the compound used to seal the joints of the piers; lead and flannel boiled in sugar, or lime and oxblood. A stroll along the aqueduct is a vertiginous experience; there is no barrier on the canal side, and the railings along the towpath are in scale with the structure itself, with generous gaps between the uprights. Far below, the Dee follows its picturesque course between wooded banks, crossed at just the right point in the composition by a three-arched bridge of 1697.

At the northern end of the aqueduct are extensive wharves and basins, laid out in anticipation of the completion of the waterway linking Chester via Wrexham to the Severn at Shrewsbury. In the event the canal, save for the spur to Llangollen, terminated here, and never quite enjoyed the commercial success hoped for. But the post-war boom in recreational navigation has revived the fortunes of what in terms of scenery and engineering achievement is one of the most fascinating waterways in the country. ■

LLANWRTYD WELLS

Reputedly the smallest town in Great Britain, Llanwrtyd was for many years a popular spa, an inland resort for the crowded industrial population of Swansea and Llanelli. The spas themselves are in an advanced state of decay, but the spruce little town continues to attract visitors, profiting from its position on the southwest-northeast trunk road through the centre of the country, its station on the mid-Wales railway line and its easy access to the uplands all around.

Llanwrtyd's hotels and boarding houses are mostly grouped around the bridge over the Irfon, at the point where the river leaves the uplands to run through a broad vale to its junction with the Wye at Builth Wells.

Hill walking, mountain biking, pony trekking and bird-watching are popular, supplemented by bizarre activities pioneered here in the 1950s like "bog-snorkelling" and a cross-country run in which men compete with horses.

> *(Llanwrtyd) Powys – Population 620*
> *Michelin Atlas p 25 or Map 503 J 27*
> *Tourist Information Centre – Ty Barcud, The Square, Llanwytyd Wells, Powys LD5 4RB.*
> ☎ *01591 610 666; Fax 01591 610 666; tic@celt.ruralwales.org*

To the southeast is the fastness of Mynydd Eppynt, while to the north the Cambrian Mountains form one of the most extensive tracts of wild landscape in all Great Britain. These rugged uplands are home to the rare red kite; the **Tourist Information Centre** has displays about this bird of prey and closed circuit TV coverage of nest activity.

■ Excursions

Abergwesyn-Tregaron Mountain Road* – *19mi/32km northwest of Llanwrtyd Wells by a steep and mostly single-track minor road to Tregaron. This road follows the old drover's route between Ceredigion (Cardiganshire) and central Wales.* ■

Craft Centre – The **Cambrian Woollen Mill** *(northern outskirts on A 483)* produces clothes and accessories, which are on sale in the shop; it was built in the early 19C, when the Welsh woollen industry was booming and is now one of only 14 surviving mills in Wales.

LLEYN PENINSULA**

Beyond the mountain masses of Snowdonia, defining the northern limit of Cardigan Bay, is this remote peninsula, where the pace of life slows and where Welshness is to be found in some of its purest forms. The hills here are rich in prehistoric remains but it is perhaps the spirit of the Celtic Church and the Middle Ages that is felt most strongly here; there are holy wells and an ancient pilgrimage route — the Saints' Way — trodden by the devout on their way from Bangor to Bardsey Island.

Despite a wonderful, sometimes dramatic coastline, tourism came late to Lleyn. The railway only ever reached as far as Pwllheli, and the attempt to turn Porth Dinllaen into the packet station for Ireland came to nothing. Even today no main road penetrates to the end of the peninsula, and it is only the south coast around Pwllheli that has been much affected

Beaches
At Aberdaron and Pwllheli Marina.

by "development". The district was one of the last in Wales to resist the pressure for the Sunday opening of pubs.

Gwynedd
Michelin Atlas p 32 or Map 503 FGH 24-25
Tourist Information Centre — Min y Don, Station Square, Pwllheli LL53 5HG
☎ 01758 613 000; Fax 01758 701 651; pwllheli.tic@gwynedd.gov.uk

■ **Sights** in clockwise order
Penarth Fawr — *Turn north off A 497 into a minor road.* Built around the mid 15C and modernised c 150 years later, Penarth Fawr is an unusually well-preserved example of a Welsh gentry house, with a spacious hall beneath a splendid timber roof.

Haven Holiday Park — *Turn south off A 497.* The great array of fun facilities — Sub-Tropical Waterworld, Go-karts, 10-pin bowling, pool tables and crazy golf — attracts day visitors as well as several thousand resident holidaymakers. The enterprise was founded as a Butlin's holiday camp in the 1930s.

Pwllheli — *At the junction of A 497 and A 499.* The principal town of the Lleyn Peninsula, Pwllheli owes much of its present prosperity as a seaside resort to the giant Butlin's leisure complex to the east.

A borough since the 14C and formerly one of North Wales' most thriving ports, Pwllheli acquired its harbour – perhaps the "salt water pool" which may be the meaning of its name in Welsh – when the sea threw a sandbank across the mouth of the River Erch. The town's maritime role declined with the rise of Porthmadog and with the coming of the railway in 1867, though today the harbour has filled up again, with more than 400 pleasure craft able to berth in the marina.

Hopes that the place would become a resort to rank with Llandudno remained unfulfilled; at the uttermost end of the Cambrian Railway, Pwllheli never really overcame its remoteness for mass holiday-making until after the Second World War. The late-19C Promenade with grand hotel and terraced boarding houses still faces southwards over the magnificent prospect of Cardigan Bay, but this West End lacks the animation of the old town, at its best on market day.

Llanbedrog – Linked to Pwllheli by a sandy beach is this little resort, sheltered by woods and hills from the west. **Plas Glyn-y-Weddw** is an extraordinary neo-Gothic mansion, built as a widow's dower house in 1856. The rooms around the great hall with its gallery, monumental staircase and triple hammerbeam roof are used for changing exhibitions of works by **contemporary Welsh artists**, though there is a semi-permanent collection too.

Abersoch – The main road (A 499) southwest from Pwllheli ends at this popular little resort, which likes to style itself 'The Welsh Riviera' (*Y Rifiera Gymreig*); on a fine day when the sea sparkles

and Abersoch's two sandy bays are full of dinghies and windsurfers the claim does not seem too fanciful. Offshore (about 2mi/3km) are St Tudwal's Islands, the abode of seals and seabirds.

Plas-yn-Rhiw★ – On a steeply-sloping site in the shelter of the Lleyn Peninsula's westernmost woodland is this endearing little country house, part Tudor, part Georgian, its **garden** lavishly stocked with plants which thrive in these protected conditions.

The house and garden were rescued in 1939 from two decades of neglect by the Misses Keating, whose love of the place still seems to pervade the modestly furnished interior and the carefully planted compartments of the garden. Eileen, Lorna and Honor worked tirelessly, not only to restore and embellish their home but to conserve the

Lleyn countryside, campaigning against the proposal for a nuclear power station, as well as buying land outright whenever the opportunity arose and presenting it, like Plas-yn-Rhiw itself, to the National Trust. Some of Honor's accomplished watercolours showing her fascination with the structure of landscape can be seen in the house.

Aberdaron – The peninsula's westernmost village looks south across its sandy bay. Just hidden by the headland is Bardsey Island, and for centuries Aberdaron was the last staging post for pilgrims on their way to the island's monastery, many of them finding refuge and sustenance in the hospice whose site is now occupied by the 17C building known as the Great Kitchen (Y Gegin Fawr). Together with the other cottages, the pair of pubs and the post office, designed by Sir Clough Williams-Ellis, it makes an attractive grouping, rare in this region of scattered farms and homesteads.

Bardsey Island★ – The Norsemen called this "the island of bards", while the Welsh name *Ynys Enlli* signifies "island of the currents". Both names are appropriate. The bards would have been the inhabitants of the **Celtic monastery**, established here perhaps as early as AD 429, their tranquillity assured (at least until the arrival of the Vikings) by the difficult passage through the tides and rips of Bardsey Sound which separates the island from the tip of the peninsula. A third title – the isle of 20 000 saints – refers to the many holy men reputed to be buried on the island. By the 13C the Celtic foundation had been taken over by the Augustinians; Bardsey was sometimes referred to as the "Welsh Rome", its remoteness making three pilgrimages here worth one to Rome itself. Pilgrims for Bardsey Island used to embark not only at Aberdaron but also at **Mwnt** north of Cardigan.

The island consists of a hill, Mynydd Enlli (548ft/167m), whose gentler western slopes are farmed, while an isthmus leads to a peninsula on which stands the lighthouse of 1821. In the 19C about 100 people lived on Bardsey, living from

© Wales Tourist Board

farming, fishing, and the making of lobster pots from willow grown in withy beds. Today's permanent population consists largely of the warden of the National Nature Reserve and a shepherd to tend the mainland sheep sent here to graze. Visitors come here on retreat, attracted by the island's monastic traditions, or to stay at the observatory, enjoying the bird life which as well as choughs includes up to 4 000 breeding pairs of the burrowing Manx shearwater. Seals may be seen offshore.

Mynydd Mawr** – Rugged enough to be called a mountain (though only 524ft/160m high), Mynydd Mawr overlooks Bardsey Island (2.5mi/4km away) across the often disturbed waters of Bardsey Sound. It makes a magnificent viewpoint; at its foot to the east the long lines of walled field boundaries suggest an ancient pattern of cultivation, while distant views take in Snowdonia, Cardigan and Caernarfon Bays, and even, in the most favourable conditions, the Wicklow Mountains in Ireland.

Porth Dinllaen* – *National Trust car park outside the golf club entrance; 15min on foot.* The headland jutting northwards into Caernarfon Bay gives a measure of protection to this bay with its sandy beach. Porth Dinllaen has a toytown look; a scatter of houses at the back of the beach, some whitewashed, some in stone, focus on the bright red pub – the *Tŷ Goch Inn.*

In the 18C and 19C Porth Dinllaen's natural advantages made it the focus of more than one attempt to develop it as the main port for the Irish mail. A glance at the map shows straight turnpike roads leading eastwards, forming part of a great highway to London which remained unbuilt, trumped by Telford's Holyhead route. A later proposal to extend the railway westward from Pwllheli met with a similar fate.

The village's tranquillity seems guaranteed following its purchase by the National Trust. ■

MACHYNLLETH*

The capital of the lower Dovey valley, this tiny town seems to have retained its intensely Welsh character despite its position at the junction of two major roads.

It was at Machynlleth in 1404 that Owain Glyn Dŵr was crowned Prince of Wales and here that he held a parliament

The **Dovey** (Dyfi) runs through one of the country's most attractive valleys; few contrasts could be greater than that between its youthful gorge high in the lonely Aran mountains and the vast expanses of tidal sand and mud, dune, marsh, fen and bog of its estuary. The "greener" forms of tourism flourish here, prompted in part by the well-established Centre for Alternative Technology *(see below)* in the valley of the Dulas, a tributary of the Dovey.

> Powys – Population 1 110
> Michelin Atlas p 25 or Map 503 I 26
> Tourist Information Centre
> – Canolfan Owain Glyndwr, Machynlleth SY20 8EE
> ☏ 01654 702 401;
> Fax 01654 703 675.

■ Sights

Celtica* – The Victorian mansion known as Plas Machynlleth now houses this ambitious "experience", which uses the most sophisticated audio-visual techniques to evoke the world of the Celts. More conventional displays on an upper floor recall the extent and achievement of the culture of the early Celts, whose history is mostly known through the records of their great opponents, the Greeks and Romans. Visitors can press a button and hear the Lord's Prayer in any one of the modern Celtic languages, either living, like Scots and Irish Gaelic, Breton, or Welsh itself, or in Manx and Cornish, which are being revived.

■ Excursions

Centre for Alternative Technology** *3mi/5km north of Machynlleth by A 487* ■

Craft Centres – A number of individual makers – woodwork, pottery, leatherwork, toys, candles, jewellery – sell their work in the **Corris Craft Centre** *(10mi/16km north by A 487)*. For woollen goods visit the **Meirion Mill Woollen Centre** *(30mi/48km south by A 470)*.

MONTGOMERY*

Apart from main roads and railways, this perfect little town seems hardly to have changed since Georgian times. Montgomery is a planned settlement, a medieval foundation, which received a Royal Charter in 1227, laid out within the protection of its castle on the ridge high above, in order to consolidate the English hold on the invasion route along the Severn valley into the heart of Wales. The strategic importance of this routeway had long been recognised; the great Iron-Age fort of **Ffridd Faldwyn** stands on the ridge a short distance away from the Norman castle, overlooking the crossing of the Severn at Rhydwhiman, close to which the Romans built their strongpoint of **Forden Gaer**.

Shortly after their Conquest of

(Trefaldwyn) Powys – Population 1 059
Michelin Atlas p 25 or Map 503 K 26

England in 1066, the Normans built a chain of castle mounds along the valley, one of them the work of Roger, a knight from Montgommeri in Normandy. Now known as **Hen Domen** (the Old Mound), this was replaced in the mid 13C by the present castle in its far stronger natural position, though town and castle retained the name of the original founder. Within its walls, which have long since disappeared, the town seems to have flourished, as market town and titular county town, until the last burst of Georgian prosperity, after which it settled into its present charming somnolence. ■

Welsh Dishes

Most traditional Welsh recipes were originally devised for maximum economy and nourishment rather than gastronomic excellence. *Cawl* is a thick broth of meat, vegetables and potatoes, still served as a standard winter meal. *Lobscaws* (pronounced Lobscouse), a stew made with left-overs, was the staple diet of poor Welsh communities in Liverpool in the 19C – hence the name "Scouse" for Liverpudlians. A mixture of hot milk and bread, sometimes thickened with an egg, *(bara-llaeth)* is unlikely to appear on many restaurant menus but a mash of swede and potatoes *(stwnsh rhwdans)* does occasionally make the transition from domestic to professional kitchen.

NEWTOWN

The settlement is aptly named Newtown, as it has enjoyed a succession of new beginnings. In 1279 a native Welsh settlement within the great bend of the Severn was replanned by Roger de Montgomery to serve as a market town. In the early 19C the rapid expansion of hand-looms and textile factories led to hopes of the place becoming a second Leeds. In the mid 20C planned expansion of industry and housing was promoted by the Mid Wales Development Corporation in order to stem the exodus from this otherwise entirely rural region.

Traces of de Montgomery's typical medieval grid plan can be distinguished in the street pattern but the dominant impression is of the 19C red brick of houses and factories, then, on the outskirts, of the modern residential estates and the 100-plus factories built here since the late 1960s.

Newtown has, however, remained relatively small; rivalry with Leeds was never realistic, and the biggest establishment at the end of the 19C was the pioneering mail-order business whose warehouse still dominates today.

(Y Drenewydd) Powys –
Population 10 548
Michelin Atlas p 25 or Map 503 K 26
Tourist Information Centre – The Park, Back Lane, Newtown SY16 2PW
☎ 01686 625 580; Fax 01686 610 065.

■ Sights

Robert Owen Memorial Museum – The reformer **Robert Owen** (1771-1858) was born in Newtown and returned here to die, though his life was spent elswhere, notably in promoting his Utopian industrial communities at New Lanark in Scotland and New Harmony, Indiana. The museum gives a good account of his life and his influence on the development of Socialism and the Co-operative movement. Owen's art nouveau **memorial tomb** is in the graveyard of the ruined **Church of St Mary**. In the 1840s St Mary's was abandoned in favour of the yellow-brick **St David's** because of the Severn's liability to flood, a situation remedied only by the recent construction of massive embankments and the building of the Clywedog Dam upstream. ■

PENRHYN CASTLE**
Gwynedd

This huge country house disguised as a Norman castle is one of the 19C's most ambitious attempts to recreate the spirit of the Middle Ages. The castle's picturesque outline of towers, curtain walls and massive keep rises above the trees of the great park occupying the peninsula ("penrhyn") protruding into the Menai Strait just east of Bangor.

The man responsible for this fantastic building complex was George Hay Dawkins Pennant (1763-1840), heir to two fortunes, one based on Jamaican sugar plantations, the other on the highly productive Penrhyn slate quarries just inland. The quarries had been developed and linked by tramway to a purpose-built harbour at the northwestern corner of the park by Richard Pennant, First Baron Penrhyn and notable late-18C "Improver", who had also transformed the estate's ancient hall-house into a castellated Gothick mansion. This edifice was incorporated into George Dawkins Pennant's new castle, begun c 1821 and completed about 13 years later. The architect was Thomas Hopper, who blended architectural motifs spanning three centuries of medieval development to

Michelin Atlas p 32 or Map 503 H 24

produce an entirely convincing if highly imaginative interpretation of a medieval stronghold. The building occupies an area of one acre/nearly half a hectare, and has a frontage of 600ft/more than 180m. More than any comparable 19C structure, Penrhyn seems ready to withstand a siege, with a keep (124ft/38m high), based on that at Castle Hedingham in Essex, a high curtain wall and four massive towers complete with murder holes. ∎

© Wales Tourist Board

PLAS NEWYDD ★★
Anglesey

In the late 18C the original hall house on the Anglesey shore of the Menai Strait was transformed into a palatial country residence by the Earl of Uxbridge. The severe, grey stone exterior conceals rooms of the greatest interest, one of them decorated with the Plas Newydd mural, the masterpiece of the inter-war artist Rex Whistler (1905-44).

Setting – The Plas Newydd estate includes 1.5mi/2.5km of the Menai coastline. The house is sited on

Michelin Atlas p 32 or Map 503 H 24

a shelf of land cut into the slope sweeping down to this noble stretch of water, with the whole of Snowdonia as an incomparable backdrop. The splendour of the situation was enhanced at the very end of the 18C by the landscape designer **Humphry Repton**, who added trees which have now reached their full magnificence. Visitors can savour this splendid setting to the full as they approach the house via a long and curving path leading downhill from the National Trust's shop and café in the former Dairy. The path also reveals a fine example of one of Anglesey's many Neolithic monuments, a cromlech, seen against the background of the extensive stable buildings. The waterside is defined by a battlemented wall with bastions and a jetty, while later additions to the grounds include an Italianate garden and extensive plantings of rhododendrons. ■

Boat Trip
From the jetty directly in front of the house (by the 3 cannons) the *Snowdon Queen* makes a return trip *(40min)* northwest as far as the Britannia Bridge; commentary on the landmarks on the shore of the Menai Straits, one of the most scenic and romantic waterways in Europe.

PLAS NEWYDD*
Denbighshire

This highly individual black-and-white house on the slopes just to the south of Llangollen was for 50 years the home of by far the most famous residents of the neighbourhood, an extraordinary couple of Irish cousins, known as the Ladies of Llangollen.

Ladies of Llangollen – The long relationship between **Lady Eleanor Butler** and **Sarah Ponsonby** caught the imagination of Regency society, which regarded their "model of perfect friendship" with a mixture of curiosity and affection. The couple, both from the upper reaches of Anglo-Irish society, first met when the orphaned Sarah, in her early teens, was languishing in boarding school. Spinster Eleanor, 16 years Sarah's senior, later came under pressure from her family to become a nun, while Sarah had to deal with the unwelcome attentions of her male guardian. A first attempt to elope, disguised as men, was frustrated but eventually, in 1778, the pair were able to leave Ireland. Finding the Vale of Llangollen "the beautifullest country in the world", they set up house here with the ostensible aim of leading a "life of sweet

Michelin Atlas p 33 or Map 503 K 25

and delicious retirement", though there is little evidence that they made any serious effort to elude the fame which their relationship, their mannish dress and their general sociability brought them. Eminent visitors were welcomed and an extensive correspondence

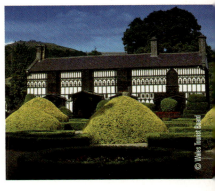

maintained, which kept them in touch with "the tattle and scandal of the world". The reign of the uncrowned Queens of Llangollen lasted for half a century; Lady Eleanor died in 1829, aged 90, and Sarah followed her partner to the grave in Llangollen churchyard two years later. ∎

PORTHMADOG

Porthmadog recalls the name of its founder, **William Madocks** (1773-1828), as well as echoing that of Prince Madog, legendary discoverer of America, who is supposed to have set sail from the estuary here in the 12C three centuries before Columbus. It reached its peak of maritime activity in the decade 1850 to 1860. In season it is a busy place, its long High Street crowded with holiday traffic making its way around the southern rim of Snowdonia, its harbour full of pleasure craft. A plume of steam announces the approach of a train along the ruler-straight embankment known as the **Cob**, for Porthmadog is the terminus of Wales' foremost narrow-gauge railway.

Porthmadog Maritime Museum – *Quayside*. An old slate shed houses the exhibits which trace the development of the harbour in 1820s, the transition from sail to steam in the 1880s, the *Western Ocean Yachts*, which contributed largely to the town's 19C prosperity; they were built in Porthmadog between 1860 and 1913, to carry slate to Germany and saltfish to Newfoundland and Labrador. There are displays of shipboard tools, sailing rigs and navigation instruments.

> Gwynedd – Population 1 675
> Michelin Atlas p 32 or Map 503 H 25
> Local map p 98
> Tourist Information Centre
> – Station Yard, Porthmadog LL49 9HW ☎ 01766 512 981; porth madog.tic@gwynedd.gov.uk

Ffestiniog Railway** – William Madocks built the Cob in 1811 in order to turn the broad estuary of the Glaslyn into profitable farmland. He thereby provided a convenient route by which a horse-powered tramway could bring its wagons loaded with slate from the Ffestiniog mines directly to the waiting sea-going ships in the harbour. Riding in "dandy-carts" on the downward journey, the horses hauled the empty wagons back up the line from 1836 until 1863, when the company acquired its first steam locomotives. By the 1920s, the Ffestiniog was making as much money from tourists as from slate, indulging in publicity which exaggerated the Alpine character of the indubitably scenic Vale of Ffestiniog. The Second World War killed both the slate and the tourist trade. The line was closed in 1946 but, thanks to the efforts of dedicated enthusiasts, the section

> **Craft Centres – Snowdon Mill Art and Craft Centre** *(signed from town centre)* is a cooperative run by makers. For woollen goods visit **Brynkir Woollen Mill** *(3.5mi/5km by A 487)*.
> **Fforwm Crefft Cymru**, Snowdon Mill Art & Craft Centre, Snowdon Street, Porthmadog LL49 9DF. ☎ 01766 510 901; Fax 10766 510 913.

across the Cob was reopened in 1955 and finally reached Blaenau Ffestiniog again in 1982.

The terminus of the Ffestiniog Railway, **Porthmadog Harbour station**, has an air of importance which the mainline station at the other end of town has lost altogether. Though largely built by volunteer labour, the line is run professionally, with automated signalling and crossings. Long trains wait in the station, perhaps headed by one of the ingenious double-ended Fairlie locomotives which enabled the railway to haul exceptionally-heavy slate trains on what is only a narrow-gauge line (2ft/600mm). The extensive station buildings include a small **Museum**; its star exhibit, apart from an 0-4-0 tank engine, is a railway hearse. The ride across the Cob is exhilarating enough but better still is the journey ever-higher through the wonderful woodlands of the **Vale of Ffestiniog**. **Plas Halt** gives access to the magnificent grounds of **Plas Tan-y-Bwlch** *(see below)*.

Near Dduallt the line reaches open mountain country and gains height by the only **rail spiral** in Britain. The barrier created by the construction of the **Tan-y-Grisiau power station** and reservoir has been triumphantly overcome, and, 13.5mi/22km after leaving Porthmadog, the line carries its passengers into what was its heartland and *raison d'être*, the slate town of **Blaenau Ffestiniog★**.

Welsh Highland Railway – Porthmadog has a second "Great Little Railway", part of the short-lived narrow-gauge line linking Porthmadog, Beddgelert and Caernarfon, which opened in the 1920s and closed soon after. Here visitors can see a station and depot, and ride a train *(45min)* on the short section of line which has been reconstructed. There are plans to re-open much more of the original line, providing public transport for inhabitants and tourists alike. ■

PORTMEIRION★★★

Gwynedd

> Michelin Atlas p 32 or Map 503 H 25

A leading luminary in the movement to conserve the environment, the architect **Sir Clough Williams-Ellis** (1883-1978) devoted much of a long lifetime to creating his own idea of the perfect environment, the dream village of Portmeirion, a serious yet inimitably playful attempt to show *"that one could develop a very beautiful site without defiling it, and given sufficient loving care, one could even improve on what God had provided"*.

Portmeirion is almost impossible to categorise. It functions as a tourist village, accommodating overnight guests in its hotel and in many of the buildings around the site. Day visitors come in large numbers, browsing among the books, Portmeirion pottery and other tasteful souvenirs on sale in several shops, patronising the café and ice-cream parlour, but mostly just enjoying the sensations of being in a place which is unique.

The village owes much to its site, a short and steep-sided valley running down through woods to the sweeping sands of the estuary of the River Dwyryd, but much more to the spirit of its creator. Sir Clough embraced modernity, building the occasional "progressive" structure such as the concrete-and-glass beach café at nearby Criccieth, but seems to have revelled more in the Baroque and Rococo, with its love of colour, theatricality, visual virtuosity, and of life as celebration and festival. The result, at Portmeirion, is akin to the sparkling fantasies of Mediterranean landscape and architecture conjured up in the murals painted at Plas Newydd by Rex Whistler *(see Index)*.

■ Tour

The approach to the village is via a long drive with trees and shrubs arranged to heighten a sense of anticipation. Even the car park, laid out on an irregular pattern and densely planted, reveals the hand of a master landscaper. The sense of arrival is further enhanced by passing through more woodland, then through the archways of **Gate House** and **Bridge House**. The eye has already been deceived by Sir Clough's illusionism and use of false perspective into thinking that these arches are much larger than they really are. The Gatehouse's mural by the Austrian artist Hans Feilbusch is only one of many decorative delights with which the village is embellished.

The **Belvedere Lookout** reveals the glorious setting of estuary and mountain, its scale in such contrast to the intimacy and intricacy of the village. At **Battery Square**, the full richness of Portmeirion begins to tell. Here are some of the earliest buildings on the site, dating from the late 1920s and early 1930s.

Beyond, dominating the Citadel area, is the **Campanile** (80ft/24m high) but looking much taller, drawing the eye skywards, then allowing it to fall to the **Piazza**, which forms the green heart of the village, the best place in which to sit and soak up the architectural wizardry on display all around. The skyline to the left of Bridge House is broken by the **Pantheon**, its dome originally made from plywood, its supports from rolled cardboard, while a nearby turret is crowned by a cupola fashioned from an upturned pig-swill boiler. Sir Clough's ambitions frequently outran his means and such expedients were common.

Below the Pantheon is the 18C **Bristol Colonnade**, rescued from that city following bomb damage, and mischievously decorated with a small bust of Sir Clough by Welsh sculptor Jonah Jones. Uphill, beyond the other delightful structures scattered along the valley rim, is a miniature **Triumphal Arch**. The Piazza is defined at its lower end by a **Gothick Pavilion**, at its upper end by the **Gloriette**, built, like much of the village, for "no useful purpose save that of looking both handsome and jolly". What seem to be jolly statues atop its flanking pillars are no more than cut-outs.

Beyond the buildings flanking the Piazza is the most substantial example of Sir Clough's magpie nature and his desire to rescue "fallen buildings", the **Town Hall**, built from fragments of a demolished Jacobean mansion.

The main path leads downwards towards the **Hotel** and the shoreline, with its **Stone Boat** moored by the quayside. Further on still are a **Camera Obscura** and **Lighthouse**. ∎

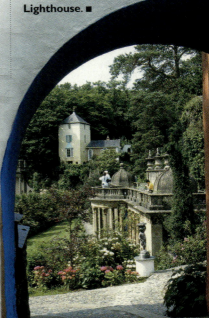

© Wales Tourist Board

POWIS CASTLE★★★
Powys

One of Wales' grandest residences, this superb building in warm red stone stands atop its ridge, buttressed by its Baroque terraced gardens, among the few to have survived anywhere in Great Britain.

■ Historical notes

The origins of the castle are obscure, though it almost certainly began as a timber fortification of the rulers of the medieval principality of Powys. By the end of the 13C century it had been rebuilt in stone and had taken on much of its present appearance. It was at this time that its lord, **Gruffudd ap Gwynwynwyn**, was obliged by Edward I to renounce his royal titles and accept the title of Baron de la Pole (= Pool or Powis). In 1587 the castle passed into the hands of **Sir Edward Herbert**, son of the Earl of Pembroke, who was responsible for much of the remodelling of the interior including the building of the Long Gallery. In 1688 his descendant, the Catholic Marquess of Powis, went into exile in France with James II, and lived at St Germain-en-Laye.

In 1722 the castle was returned to the family, into which **Edward**

Michelin Map p 25 or Map 503 K 26

Clive, son of **Clive of India**, later married. In 1804 Clive was granted the title of Earl of Powis, and spent much of his huge fortune in restoring the neglected castle and filling it with fine paintings and furniture as well as with the family's unsurpassed private collection of Indian artefacts. It was at this time that Sir Robert Smirke was employed to romanticise the castle's outline. At the beginning of the 20C another eminent architect, **GF Bodley**, undertook major alterations, while the Fourth Earl's wife embellished the gardens. In 1952 Powis Castle was given to the National Trust.

■ Tour

Exterior – The sandstone castle, known justifiably in Welsh as Y Castell Coch ("The Red Castle") enjoys a magnificent position on the gritstone ridge which rises grandly over extensive parklands. Seen from the lower ridge to the southeast, its outline, with chimneys, battlements and regular window patterning, is unmistakable. The castle's core is arranged around a small inner court. The principal entrance up to the late

18C was the East Gate facing towards Welshpool, but the main approach today is from the west, through a narrow medieval gateway and on to the great **forecourt** with its splendid Baroque lead statue of Fame.

Interior – This comprises what is often considered to be the finest suite of rooms in Wales.

Ground Floor – An appropriately grandiose beginning is provided by the **Great Staircase** (c 1675-85), probably the work of William Winde who had built the family's London house. The *grisaille* wall paintings of the lower hall seem pale in comparison with the ceiling, painted by Verrio in imitation of *The Triumph of Venice* by Veronese. Verrio's pupil Gerard Lanscroon was responsible for the wall paintings.

First Floor – Rows of books climb high on the tall walls of the **Library**, the paintings even higher. The ceiling painting is by Lanscroon, the delicate **miniature of Lord Herbert of Cherbury** by Isaac Oliver (d 1617). It shows the subject resting pensively in a landscape not wholly unlike that to be seen through the windows of several of the rooms on this floor.

The **Oak Drawing Room** was the centrepiece of Sir Edward Herbert's late-16C scheme of improvements, though again the splendid plasterwork and linenfold panelling is the work of Bodley. There is an unmistakable portrait of Charles II by Kneller and a Bellotto of the Adige at Verona, bought by Clive of India in 1771.

The **State Bedroom**, an "extraordinary and extravagant casket of a room" (R Haslam), is unique in Brit-

ain in having the Versailles arrangement of a balustrade protecting the bed area from the crowd attending the levee of its eminent occupant.

The magnificent T-shaped **Long Gallery** is the only one of Sir Edward Herbert's rooms to remain intact; above its *trompe l'œil* wainscoting is an array of Herbert coats of arms and a fine plaster ceiling. The splendid items of furniture include gilt console tables bearing sculptures, one of which is a rare Roman marble of the 1C BC of a snarling **Cat** and writhing **Snake**.

Leading from the gallery are the State Bathroom, the Walcot Room with a bed made – possibly by Bodley – of crudely-carved 17C panels, and the Gallery Room with fine examples of Empire furniture. The Duke's Room with Brussels tapestries and the Lower Tower Bedroom are contained within the castle's western towers.

The **Blue Drawing Room** with more Brussels tapestries, panelling of about 1660, and a ceiling by Lanscroon, has remained unaltered since the start of the 18C.

At the foot of the servants' staircase, the Billiard Room has an amazing array of traditionally stuffed and mounted birds.

Ballroom Range – These rooms bear the stamp of the Clive family, the Ballroom itself being originally hung with Clive of India's picture collection. *Lord Clive Receiving the Grant of the Diwani from the Great Mogul* by Benjamin West is full of fanciful pageantry, its impact equalled by that of the superb Tournai tapestry showing a Venetian embassy to Cairo. The most extraordinary object, in the **Tent Room**, is the reconstruction of part of **Tipu Sahib's tent**.

Beyond the Ballroom is the **Clive Museum**, recently fitted out with a masterly set of **showcases**, designed entirely in the spirit of British India, in which is displayed the fascinating **Clive Collection** of Indian and Far Eastern works of art, arms and armour.

Gardens – The dramatically terraced gardens are the finest example in Britain of a kind of landscaping that was all but obliterated in the 18C by fashionable enthusiasm for the informal style which took Nature, rather than architecture, as its model.

The designer of the gardens and their exact date are unknown but they are characteristic of the taste of the late 17C. The sojourn of the exiled Marquess of Powis in France must have influenced their layout; in the mid 18C the antiquary Thomas Pennant refers to the family's penchant for copying "the wretched taste of St Germain-en-Laye" but the real inspiration must be the great Renaissance gardens of Italy, where villas and their surroundings were boldly laid out on the steepest of slopes. ■

RHUDDLAN CASTLE★★
Denbighshire

Even deprived of their battlements, the stout towers of Rhuddlan Castle still stand confidently on the low rise above the Clwyd, the river diverted by Edward I's engineers to enable his new fortress to be supplied directly from the sea.

Michelin Atlas p 33 or Map 503 J 24

■ Historical notes

Rhuddlan was the second of the great castles, after Flint, to be built in the course of Edward I's subjugation of North Wales, but invaders had been this way before.

The Saxons had founded a settlement here. In 1073 the Norman known as Robert of Rhuddlan had thrown up a **castle mound**, known as **Twthill**, still prominent on its site just to the south of the later stronghold; it was accompanied by a planned town of which some earthworks remain.

The fordability of the Clwyd was the principal determinant of the castle's location, but the river had to be led into a new bed to conform to the plans of Edward's architect, the Savoyard James of St George. For three years from 1277 onwards, diggers from the Fens and elsewhere laboured to excavate the new channel (2mi/3km long) as the castle walls took shape on the slope above. In 1282 Rhuddlan formed the main base of operations for the attack on Snowdonia. A **bastide town** (minus walls) was laid out, its outline still evident in the street pattern of the small modern town.

Ruins – The most prominent part of the castle ruins is the **West Gatehouse**. This was one of two gatehouses guarding the castle's inner ward, diamond-shaped in plan, and with single towers at the other two corners.

The only trace remaining of such substantial timber structures as the Queen's Hall and King's Hall are foundations, beam holes and roof creases. Edward's first wife, Queen Eleanor, had a garden made in the courtyard, laid with 6 000 turves and with seats around a fishpond surrounding the well.

The lower towers and walls of the outer ward descended to the river, where there was a dock. A dry moat ran round the remainder of the walls. ■

RHYL

(Y Rhyl) Denbighshire

At the beginning of the 19C what is now a popular resort was no more than a collection of fishermen's huts at the point where the Clwyd finds its way to the sea through a broad belt of marshland. Development began in earnest after 1848 when the railway arrived, and Rhyl soon joined the ranks of the other watering places of the north coast, with a promenade, pier, winter garden, respectable terraces of hotels and boarding houses, and a medley of churches and chapels, including St Thomas' by Sir Gilbert Scott with its landmark steeple. Pier and winter garden have gone, accommodation is now mostly in flatlets and caravans, and bingo halls and amusement arcades stud the townscape.

> **Parking** – There is an underground car park beneath the Promenade.

The town is, however, committed to reversing what had been perceived as a decline and has invested heavily in new facilities to cater for the more sophisticated demands made nowadays by its traditional Merseyside and Lancashire clientele.

> *Michelin Atlas p 33 or Map 503 J 24 – Population 24 909*
> *Tourist Information Centres*
> *– Rhyl Children's Village, West Parade, Rhyl LL18 1HZ ☏ 01745 355 068; Fax 01745 3442 255.*
> *Offa's Dyke Centre, Central Beach, Prestatyn LL19 7EY*
> *☏ 01745 889 092.*

Promenade – Rhyl's Promenade (2mi/3km long) overlooks a sandy beach which at low tide seems to extend to the horizon. At its western end, fishing boats mingle with recreational craft at the mouth of the Clwyd.

A stroll eastwards brings the visitor into tempting contact with one attraction after another – Ocean Beach Amusement Park, Activity Centre for teenagers, Waterpark, Skytower (240ft/73m), paddling pools and a Children's Village. A sparkling new focal point has been created in the open-air Events Arena (capacity 8 000) which is sheltered from sea breezes. It is flanked to the west by the big blue barn of the **Sea Life Aquarium**. ∎

ST ASAPH

The city of St Asaph consists of little more than the single street climbing from the five-arched bridge over the River Elwy to the low rise on which stands the smallest of Britain's cathedrals.

(Llanelwy) Denbighshire – Population 3 399
Michelin Atlas p 33 or Map 503 J 24

■ Cathedral★

The simplicity of the square-towered edifice seems to proclaim its affinity with the Celtic monastery founded here in AD 560 by St Kentigern, also known as St Mungo, Bishop of Strathclyde, and led later by his successor, St Asaph.

The present building was begun in the early 13C but its history is one of frequent destruction followed by restoration and further building. Its present appearance is in part due to the extensive restoration carried out by Sir Gilbert Scott in the second half of the 19C. The cathedral has survived several attempts to transfer the diocese to other locations, in the late 13C to Rhuddlan, in the 16C to Denbigh, and later to Bangor. In the post-Reformation period it was a great centre of Welsh learning.

Interior – Despite its relatively small dimensions, the interior conveys an atmosphere of great spaciousness and calm, and achieves the dignity and presence appropriate to a cathedral. There is much bare stone and little ornamentation; the nave arcades have no capitals, though there are medieval carved corbels supporting the timber roof of the nave. In the choir are late-15C canopied stalls, the only ones of their kind in Wales. Bishop Morgan is buried beneath the throne, while his Bible and other literary treasures are displayed in an alcove by the Chantry Chapel. ■

SNOWDONIA ★★★
(Eryri) Gwynedd and Conwy

> *Michelin Atlas p 32-33 or Map 503 H-I 24-25*

The vast and mountainous area of North Wales takes its name from its highest peak, Snowdon (3 560ft/1 085m) which, in the opinion of many, is the most beautiful mountain in England and Wales. The approach to this heartland is guarded by other mountain ramparts like Cadair Idris overlooking the Mawddach and Dysynni valleys far to the south. Virtually identical to the ancient kingdom of Gwynedd, Snowdonia was a seat of rebellion which had to be secured for England by a chain of mighty castles. It is still a stronghold of Welshness. Until the 16C the area stayed remote, roamed by wolves and bears. The economy remained tied to the meagre yields of upland agriculture, until the quickening pace of life in the 18C and early 19C brought both industry – in the form of mineral and slate extraction – and tourists in search of 'picturesque and sublime' scenery.

Snowdonia National Park – The second-largest National Park in England and Wales, which was established in 1951, extends over the greater part of the mountainous area. Its name in Welsh, *Eryri*, means Place of Eagles, although there are no eagles now. With its unrivalled combination of glorious mountain ranges and a splendid coastline, Snowdonia depends on tourism for much of its livelihood. Most visitors come for the day, from resorts on the north coast or from Snowdonia's own coastline on Cardigan Bay but climbers and serious walkers prefer to stay in one of the small towns or villages within the Park.

The Mountains – Snowdonia's geology is varied and complex. The oldest rocks, from the Cambrian period of c 600 million years ago, form the resistant and rugged Rhinog range. Cadair Idris, the Aran and Arenig mountains, as well as Snowdon itself owe their origin to outbursts of volcanic activity in Ordovician times, while the slate rocks which have contributed so much to the appearance and economy of parts of Snowdonia were formed as a result of the Silurian earth movements, which also gave the Scottish mountains their basic structure.

The decisive force which shaped the surface of the landscape seen today was the **ice**, which advanced and receded across the area for a period lasting some 70 000 years and which beat its final retreat only some 10 000 years ago. The slopes of both Snowdon and Cadair Idris were sculpted by glaciers into spectacular cwms separated by almost razor-sharp ridges, their depths filled with the glacial **lakes** that are one of the glories of the Park.

The Valleys – The mountain blocks are divided by valleys, many of which were ground into characteristic U-shapes by the action of the glaciers, leaving the hanging valleys typical of this kind of country, a phenomenon developed to perfection in the Pass of Llanberis and the Nant Ffrancon valley. The rivers form many attractive stretches; the Conwy and its tributaries around Betws-y-Coed are marked by a series of waterfalls, while the defile of the Glaslyn at Aberglaslyn is one of the famous sights of Snowdonia.

The northern and southern peaks are separated by the lush landscapes of the **Vale of Ffestiniog** beside the River Dwyryd. Here is situated **Plas Tan-y-Bwlch**, the residential study centre of the Snowdonia National Park, set in magnificent and picturesque grounds. It can be reached by the road or the Blaenau-Ffestiniog Railway. The slate quarries and waste tips of Blaenau Ffestiniog were tactfully excluded from the National Park when its boundaries were being drawn.

■ **Northern Snowdonia**

This is Snowdonia proper, centred on Snowdon itself, but including other ranges like the Carneddau and the Glyders, as well as outstanding individual peaks like shapely Moel Hebog (2 566ft/782m) and sharply pointed Cnicht (2 264ft/690m) rising on either side of the Pass of Aberglaslyn.

Snowdon★★★ – The Great Mound (*Yr Wyddfa*) is the Welsh name for Snowdon, the "snowy height" marvelled at by the early Anglo-Saxons who no doubt first saw the wintry mountain from the relative safety of the sea.

Snowdon has been compared in shape to a starfish or Catherine wheel. From the summit, a series of ridges extends outwards, precipitous cwms dividing one from another. In places the ridges rise to form subordinate peaks like Moel Eilio to the northwest or Yr Aran to the south.

Visitor Centres – Information Centres run by the Snowdonia National Park Authority are situated in Betws-y-Coed *(see p 32)*, Blaenau Ffestiniog *(see p 34)*, Dolgellau *(see p 47)*, Harlech *(see p 54)*.

Other Tourist information centres are located in Bala, Barmouth, Conwy, Corris, Llanberis *(see p 60)*, Porthmadog and Tywyn.

The **Residential Study Centre** at Plas Tan-y-Bwlch near Porthmadog provides courses on a great variety of activities related to the natural features of the National Park.

Snowdon Sherpa Bus Service – The service, which helps to ease congestion in the Park by enabling visitors to leave their cars behind, operates throughout the year but more frequently in summer. Timetables are available from the Snowdonia National Park Information Centres and Tourist Information Centres.

Weather Conditions – A 24hr **weather forecast** is available on Mountaincall Snowdonia ☎ 0891 500 449. Mountain walkers should bear in mind that temperatures drop rapidly as height is gained, roughly by 2 C for every 1 000ft/300m. This, combined with wind-chill, can mean that summit conditions can be unpleasantly, even dangerously, different from those which seemed so encouraging at the starting point of a climb down in the valley. The upper sections can be treacherous in wet or icy conditions and snow can fall in Snowdonia not only in winter but at any time of the year.

Emergency – In the case of injury telephone ☎ 999 and ask for the police.

Ascent of Snowdon – Climbing to the summit of Snowdon or any other peak in Snowdonia requires exactly the same precautions and equipment as any other mountain walk and should not be undertaken lightly. There is a **mountain rescue post** at the western end of Llyn Ogwen. Information on appropriate equipment is available from the Snowdonia National Park Information Centres *(see above)*.

Most of the different **paths or tracks leading to the summit** are described in the text below. Lurking beneath the summit is a café, successor to a hotel, much decried by purists, but a welcome source of hot drinks and other refreshments nevertheless.

The **National Mountain Centre**, at Plas-y-Brenin near Capel Curig *(west of Betwys-y-Coed by A 5)*, offers expert tuition to individuals and groups in various aspects of mountaineering (abseiling, rock climbing. ice climbing, indoor climbing, orienteering, skiing) and canoeing (white water, kayak). ☎ 01690 720 280; Fax 01690 720 394.

As is to be expected, the **panorama** from the summit, in clear conditions, is outstanding, encompassing most of North Wales and perhaps reaching to the Isle of Man, the Lake District, and even the Wicklow Mountains in Ireland. **Paths to the summit** – The highest mountain south of the Scottish border inevitably attracts numerous admirers and would-be conquerors.

The **Snowdon Mountain Railway**** is rarely short of passengers, as it climbs doggedly up the long ridge from Llanberis but the footpaths to the summit are also well trodden.

Parallel with the railway up the north face runs the **Llanberis Path** (5mi/8km) which is generally considered to be the most popular footpath to the top, if not the most exciting.

Another relatively easy path is the **Snowdon Ranger Path**, which approaches the summit from the west above Llyn Dwellyn (A 4085) and can be combined with the Rhyd Ddu Path for the descent.

Perhaps the most rewarding approach to the summit is via the **Pyg Track**, which climbs up the east face starting at a relatively high point (1 168ft/356m) from the large car park at Pen-y-Pass (A 4086) near the southern end of the Pass of Llanberis; it gives a fine vista down the whole length of the pass towards Anglesey and ends with a strenuous zigzag haul to the summit. The descent can be varied from the bottom of the zigzag by branching off down the **Miners' Track**, which drops abruptly to Llyn Glaslyn and then more gently to Llyn Llydaw with old copper workings much in evidence along the way.

The **Watkin Path**, up the south face starting from Pont Bethania (A 498) in the Nant Gwynant valley, is perhaps the most arduous of the Snowdon paths, since it involves a long climb (3 300ft/over 1 000m), virtually the whole height of the mountain. By way of compensation, the lengthy climb passes fine waterfalls, the rock where the 84-year-old Gladstone spoke in defence of the rights of small nations, and the waste tips and structures abandoned long ago by the slate quarries which once ate away at the mountain. The views of the great embayment formed by Snowdon, Yr Aran and Craig-ddu are superb.

Far more of a challenge than any of these walks is the famous **Snowdon Horseshoe**, an airy ridge-top scramble which takes those with no fear of heights around the great crescent enclosing Llyn Glaslyn and Llyn Llydaw. This exhilarating excursion begins at Pen-y-Pass, proceeds at snail's pace along the razor-sharp ridge of **Crib Goch**, takes in the summit of Snowdon and returns along the ridge top leading to Y Lliwedd.

Only in a few places is it possible for more passive observers to get an overall view of the mountain, though the range can easily be circumnavigated on main roads. One of the **grandest vistas** opens up for motorists driving west along the road (A 4086) from Capel Curig; another can be enjoyed from a lay-by off the road (A 498) near the head of the Nant Gwynant valley.

Carnedd Range – This block of mountains fills a vast area between the sea, the Vale of Conwy and the Nant Ffrancon valley. **Carnedd Llewelyn** (3 485ft/1 064m) and **Carnedd Dafydd** (3 423ft/1 044m) are the second and third highest mountains in Snowdonia, part of a spine of mostly rounded grassy summits running north-south with subsidiary ridges branching off and enclosing lakes, most of which are now used as reservoirs. The streams fed by these lakes run eastward to the Conwy, their final steep sections forming waterfalls in places. It is, however, to the north that one of Wales' most

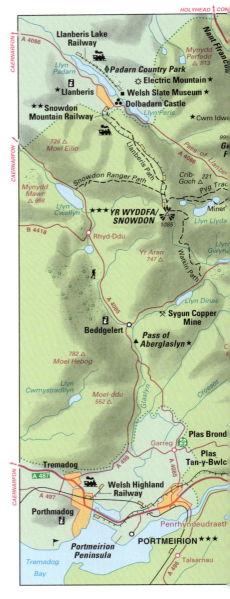

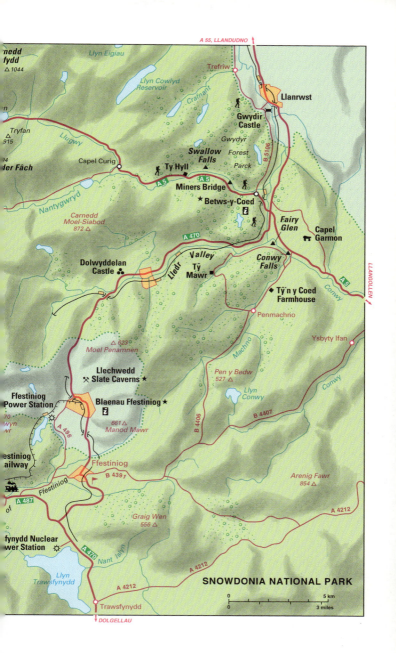

spectacular falls is found, Rhaeadr Fawr or **Aber Falls** (200ft/60m), at the point where the River Goch crashes over a barrier formed by hard igneous rock.

Just outside the National Park boundary to the north, the great rock buttress of **Penmaenmawr** projects into Conwy Bay, for centuries a formidable barrier to travellers along the coast, now overcome by the railway and the road (A 55). Made of quartz dolerite, the headland has been gnawed away for years for roadstone, the quarry operations contributing adversely to the allure of the little resort of Penmaenmawr, which was once a favourite with Gladstone.

Away from the coast, the Carneddau have a brooding, solitary atmosphere. No roads penetrate the interior of the massif, though the Roman highway from Canovium (Caerhun) to Segontium just outside Caernarfon crossed the pass at Bwlch y Ddeufaen, a route followed by today's bunched powerlines. Some idea of the grandeur of these mountains can be gained from the Iron-Age fort of **Pen-y-Gaer**, superbly located high above the Vale of Conwy and reached by a steep minor lane from the road (B 5106) near Dolgarrog.

The Glyders and Nant Ffrancon – The southwestern rim of the Carnedd range drops abruptly to **Nant Ffrancon**, the spectacular U-shaped valley which, with its cwms, rock bars, moraines and perched rocks, provided 19C British geologists with conclusive evidence about the effects of glaciation on landforms. The floor of the lower valley was once filled by a lake, whose disappearance has left a flat surface across which the River Ogwen meanders. At the exit from the valley are the huge **Penrhyn Quarries**; below them lies their dependent town of **Bethesda**, like Blaenau Ffestiniog built on and out of slate.

The valley has long provided a route of some kind through the mountains, described in the 18C as "the most dreadful horse path in Wales". Telford improved the situation, his splendidly-engineered Holyhead road still the basis of

© Wales Tourist Board

today's highway (A 5). The arch of the old packhorse bridge can still be seen beneath the later bridge below **Ogwen Cottage**. Here, at the western end of the gloomy waters of **Llyn Ogwen**, is a youth hostel and mountain rescue post, the starting point for climbers and walkers on their way up the dramatically-gouged northern flanks of the Glyder range. Britain's first National Nature Reserve, **Cwm Idwal***, "a monument to ice", was designated here in 1954, to protect the crags and cliffs around the great cleft of the **Devil's Kitchen**, the glacial lake of **Llyn Idwal**, and the arctic-alpine flora, which makes a glorious late-spring and early-summer display, at least in those areas inaccessible to sheep. The rocks here present the kind of challenge which made them a training ground for the ascent of far higher peaks.

Some of the finest walks in Snowdonia make use of the different approaches to the summits here, which include Y Garn (3 104ft/ 946m), **Glyder Fawr** (3 279ft/ 999m) and **Glyder Fach** (3 262ft/ 994m), where the frost-shattered rocks are piled into strange formations like the Cantilever and the **Castle of the Winds**. **Tryfan** (3 010ft/915m) is supposed to be the only peak in Wales which cannot be climbed without using one's hands. Beyond Llyn Ogwen to the east, the road (A 5) leads to **Capel Curig**, overlooked from the south by the beautiful elongated shape of Moel Siabod (2 861ft/872m). Capel Curig is famous, less for the Celtic holy man who gave the place his name than for **Plas y Brenin**, long-established as a school for the mastery of mountaineering technique, now the official National Mountain Centre.

■ Southern Snowdonia

The National Park extends southwards beyond Cadair Idris to overlook the mouth of the Dovey *(Dyfi)*, one of the three splendid estuaries which penetrate the mountains and add greatly to their appeal. Between the outlets of the rivers is a fine coastline, in part formed by the lower ranges of the mountains themselves, which are traversed by corniche-like main roads, and in part consisting of coastal flats and sand dunes with fine west-facing beaches, a unique feature in a British National Park. Inland, apart from Cadair Idris and perhaps the Rhinogs, the mountains are less visited than northern Snowdonia, and walks of great solitude and splendour are still possible.

Cadair Idris*** — Although the great "Chair (or Throne) of Idris" (2 928ft/892m) is just the third highest peak in Snowdonia, its majestic presence is surpassed only by Snowdon itself. Cadair Idris dominates the country to the south of Dolgellau, though its character is best appreciated from some distance away, such as the **Precipice Walk** *(see p 47)* or close to. A drive along the minor road from Dolgellau to the exquisite little **Cregennen Lakes** reveals something of the mountain's grandeur, and it is also possible to ascend from this northern side.

The finest approach to Cadair Idris on foot, though not the easiest, is undoubtedly by the **Minfordd Path**, which begins on the southeastern flank of the mountain, just north of Tal-y-llyn Lake. A steep climb through ancient oak woods leads across rugged open country to one of the most awe-inspiring sights in Snowdonia, **Llyn Cau**, its dark waters held in a great cauldron of cliffs. This was the scene that the painter **Richard Wilson** quite unnecessarily, sought to improve upon in his famous picture of 1774, by re-ordering the various elements of the composition and adding a precipice. The climb to the summit slowly ascends the rim of the cauldron, the reward being a superb **panorama** over the valley of the Mawddach towards Snowdon to the north and to the rolling heights of mid-Wales to the south. The return is by the same route. ■

TYWYN

Between the estuaries and sand bars of the Dysynni to the north and the Dovey (Dyfi) to the south is Tywyn with its two sites – the modest modern family resort facing a long stretch (6mi/10km) of sandy beach and the older core lying a mile inland.

Beaches – At Tywyn and Aberdyfi.
Old Twywn – The focus is a small square with a pair of big hotels and a confident Assembly Rooms (1897), now a cinema. Here too is the ancient **Church of St Cadfan**, mostly of Norman date. Cadfan was a Christian missionary from Brittany, who founded a monastery here early in the 6C; dating from the 8C, the so-called Cadfan Stone in the church bears an inscription whose interpretation is disputed, but which is almost certainly the earliest example of written Welsh.
Talyllyn Railway* – This narrow-gauge line, originally opened in 1866 and closed in 1950, was the first to receive the loving attentions of railway preservation enthusiasts, among them the Reverend Awdry, writer and prolific creator of steam locomotives with human characteristics like Thomas the Tank Engine. When the preservationists took over in 1951, the track, according to one account, was held together only by the grass that had grown through the sleepers.

The trains chuff their way through pretty valley scenery, crossing an imposing brick-and-stone viaduct, depositing sightseers at the Dolgoch Falls *(see below)*, and terminating in the forest at Nant Gwernol (about 8mi/12km inland). Because this is the most senior of preserved lines, its **museum** at Tywyn has much railway material which might not otherwise have found a home. ∎

Gwynedd – Population 3 028
Michelin Atlas p 24 or Map 503 H 26
Tourist Information Centre – High Street, Tywyn LL36 9AD
☏ *01654 710 070; Fax 01654 710 070; tywyn.tic@gwynedd.gov.uk*
Snowdonia National Park Information Centre – The Wharf Gardens, Aberdyfi LL35 0ED ☏ */Fax 01654 767 321.*

VALLE CRUCIS ABBEY*
Denbighshire

The substantial ruins of this abbey are set in a wild and until recently quite unspoiled valley, a characteristic location for the Cistercians who came here in 1201.

Valle Crucis was the last of the 14 Cistercian monasteries in Wales but became one of its richest. Its founder, buried here on his death in 1236, was Madog ap Gruffudd Maelor, an ancestor of Owain Glyn Dŵr and ally of Llywelyn the Great. In its heyday the abbey was a centre of learning and literature, associated with the poets Iolo Goch and Guto'r Glyn. By the end of the 15C the abbots had acquired a taste for good living; the last but one of their number brought disgrace on the Order through shady property deals and was imprisoned in the Tower of London. By the time of the Dissolution, the community had been reduced to a mere six monks.

Michelin Atlas p 33 or Map 503 K 25 – 2mi/3km north of Llangollen by A 542

In the years that followed, the abbey was robbed for its stone and lead, while parts were converted into dwelling houses and farm buildings. Restoration began as early as the mid-19C, when archeological investigations began and Sir Gilbert Scott repaired the abbey's most distinctive feature, its splendid west front.

Firmly set on the valley floor, the abbey ruins are first seen against a background of steep and shaggy slopes rising above the little River Eglwyseg. The stream supplied fresh water and fed one of the essential components of the monastic economy, the fishpond, which still remains, the only one of its kind in Wales. ∎

LAKE VYRNWY★
Powys

Fed by streams draining from the remote high country on the borders of Powys and Gwynedd, the waters of this great reservoir are held back by the first large masonry dam to be built in Britain. In the late 19C, the valley community of Llanwddyn, a village of several dozen houses, had to give way to the imperatives of water supply for the thirsty city of Liverpool. Completed between 1881 and 1888, Lake Vrynwy supplies Liverpool with water via a conduit (68mi/110km long).

Michelin Atlas p 33 or Map 503 J 25
Tourist Information Centre – Unit 2, Vyrnwy Craft Workshops, Lake Vyrnwy SY10 0LY ☎ 01691 870 346.

Visitor Centre – A multi-media display tells the tale of the area in the words of Wddyn the Wise, a holy recluse who by tradition dwelt in a cell by a local waterfall. ■

WELSHPOOL*

The market town of Welshpool stands in the deep valley of the Lledan Brook close to its confluence with the Severn. In touch with the English lowlands as well as with the Welsh interior, it has long been the focal point of communication routes; two roads lead westward, one via Llanfair Caereinion to Dolgellau and southern Snowdonia, the other via Newtown to Machynlleth. The Montgomeryshire Canal arrived in 1797, the mainline railway in 1860, the narrow-gauge line to Llanfair Caereinion in 1903.

Together with Llanfyllin, the town is one of the two planned boroughs laid out in the mid 13C by Gruffudd ap Gwynwynwyn, Prince of Powys. **Pool Street,** divided into Broad, High and Mount Streets, formed the principal axis of the medieval town, running from the central crossroads and curving gently to climb the ridge whose

(Y Trallwng) Powys – Population 5 900
Michelin Atlas p 25 or Map 503 K 26
Tourist Information Centre – Vicarage Garden, Church Street, Welshpool SY21 7DD ☎ 01938 552 043; Fax 01938 554 038.

prolongation southwards made an excellent defensive site for Powis Castle *(see p 88).* The character of the street is attractively mixed, mainly Georgian and Victorian but with some obviously older buildings and a pleasing variety of materials, including brick, timber framing and the local grey-green sandstone. The street would be periodically filled with the bleating of countless sheep, brought to what was (and still is) the biggest one-day **sheep market** in Europe, though the market itself has long been removed to a less cramped site. ■

WREXHAM

This busy town, the largest in North Wales, stands at the centre of a sprawling district which grew up around the local industries of coal and iron. Wrexham seems to have flourished at most periods of its existence.

Beginning as a village, it exploited its position between lowlands to the east and mountainous country to the west, becoming an important market town in the Middle Ages. The mineral-rich uplands enhanced its prosperity in the 18C and 19C, but enthusiasm for industrial progress led to desertion by the gentry who had hitherto made Wrexham the focus of their social activity. Not one of their town mansions remains; of the fine country houses, which once stood in a more or less complete ring around the town, Erddig alone survives, recently rescued from mining subsidence.

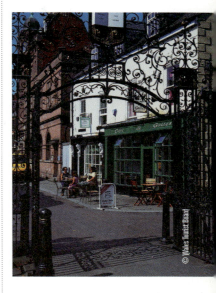

Wrexham still has its magnificent parish church, one of the "Seven Wonders of Wales"; after much ill-advised demolition the town centre is well cared for and efforts are being made to open up the fascinating industrial heritage of the hinterland. ■

(Wrecsam) Wrexham
– Population 39 929
Michelin Atlas p 33 or Map 503 L 24
Local map see p 68
Tourist Information Centre
– Lambpit Street, Wrexham LL11 1WN ☎ 01978 292 015; Fax 01978 292 467; tic@wrexham.gov.uk

PRACTICAL INFORMATION

■ Planning a trip ■

Seasons – Summer is the best time for visiting Wales and enjoying its natural attractions on the coast or in the mountains. Spring and autumn are good seasons for visiting parks and gardens when the flowers are in bloom or the leaves are turning colour. The tourist season, when the main festivals are held, runs from Easter to October. At any time of year there is the possibility of rain, owing to the mountains and the prevailing westerly wind; in winter there may be snow, especially on the high ground.

The **Wales Tourist Board** provides assistance in planning a trip to Wales and an excellent range of brochures and maps.

Wales Tourist Board, Brunel House, 2 Fitzalan Road, Cardiff CF24 0UY; ☏ 029 2047 5226 (brochures); ☏ 029 2049 9909 (switchboard); Fax 029 2047 5345; info@tourism.wales.gov.uk; www.visitwales.com

North Wales Tourism: 77 Conway Road, Colwyn Bay LL29 7LN; ☏ 01492 531 731; Fax 01492 530 059; croeso@nwt.co.uk; www. nwt.co.uk

Mid-Wales Tourism: The Station, Machynlleth SY20 8TG; ☏ 0800 273 7 47 (freephone); ☏ 01654 702 653; Fax 01654 703 235; mwt@mid-wales-tourism.org.uk; www.mid-wales-tourism.org.uk

Wales Information Bureau, British Visitor Centre, 1 Lower Regent Street, London SW1 4XT; ☏ 020 8846 9000 (British Tourist Authority); 020 7808 3838 (Enquiries about Wales).

There are **Tourist Information Centres** in all parts of the country with information on sightseeing, accommodation, places to eat, transport, entertainment, sports and local events. They are usually well signed but some are open only during the summer season; addresses and telephone numbers are given in each chapter.

■ Getting there ■

By Air – Cardiff-Wales airport (12mi/19km west of Cardiff city centre) at Rhoose in the Vale of Glamorgan has daily scheduled flights to a number of cities in the UK, Ireland and continental Europe with world-wide connections via Manchester and Amsterdam. The international airports at Manchester and Birmingham are accessible from many parts of Wales and London Heathrow is 140mi/225km from Cardiff via the M 4 motorway.

Information, brochures and timetables are available from the airlines and from travel agents. Many airlines organise fly-drive facilities.

Three major airports serve passengers travelling to Wales; two are just over the border in England; Cardiff and Birmingham offer long-term parking
- Cardiff Airport ☏ 01446 711 111;
- Birmingham International Airport ☏ 0121 767 5511;
- Manchester Airport ☏ 0161 489 3000;

– Fairwood Airport near Swansea (a smaller airport for light aircraft) ☏ 01792 468 321 (Swansea TIC).

By Rail – Fast rail services link major towns in South and North Wales with London and other English cities and also connect with ferry services to and from Fishguard and Holyhead.

By Bus and Coach – A network of express coach services run by a number of operators covers most of Wales. North and South Wales are linked by the TrawsCambria line between Cardiff, Aberystwyth and Bangor. Details available from Tourist Information Centres and local bus stations. Connections to the rest of Great Britain are run by National Express.

National Express, Birmingham; ☏ 08705 808 080 (National call centre); ☏ 0121 625 1122; Fax 0121 456 1397 (Head Office); www.gobycoach.com

■ Motoring ■

South Wales is linked to the national motorway network by the M 4 motorway while a highway of near-motorway standard, the North Wales Expressway, connects the towns and resorts of the north coast to the north of England. Main roads generally are well engineered and relatively uncrowded, though the nature of the country imposes many bends and steep gradients. Special care needs to be taken on minor roads, especially in mountainous areas and in other places where grazing animals may be a hazard.

■ Places to stay ■

It is advisable to book well in advance for the holiday season.

Booking service – Most Tourist Information Centres will arrange accommodation for a small fee. Room prices, even for a double room, may be quoted per person.

Publications – Most Tourist Information Centres provide, free of charge, an information booklet listing hotels, bed and breakfast and other accommodation in their area. The **Wales Tourist Board** (see p 110) publishes a number of magazines (free of charge) which provide a selection of hotels, guesthouses, farmhouse accommodation, self-catering properties and caravan parks:

Wales Countryside Holidays and *Wales Farm Holidays*.

Hotels – There is a full range of hotel accommodation from the most expensive and formal to smaller and more modest establishments. Accommodation guides are available from Tourist Information Centres. See below for some suggestions.

The two rates quoted for each establishment refer to the nightly rate of a single or double room. Breakfast may not always be included in the price. Some restaurants listed below may also have rooms.

ABERDOVEY

Penhelig Arms, Aberdovey, LL35 0LT, ☎ 01654 767215; info@penheligarms.com – £45-£94. Standing by the harbour, looking across Dyfi Estuary, this part 18C hotel is comfortably furnished, particularly in the superior bedrooms. There are views from most rooms. Cosy restaurant offering strongly seafood-based menus, some of it local.

Preswylfa, Garth Rd, LL35 0LE, ☎ 01654 767239; info@preswylfa.co.uk – £50-£70. Edwardian house overlooking Cardigan Bay, Dyfi Estuary. Fushia pink drawing room with piano for those who wish to tinker. Fresh, light rooms; simple but tasteful furniture. Organic food served on well-spaced, linen-clad tables in sunny dining room.

Brodawel, Tywyn Rd, LL35 0SA, ☎ 01654 767347; info@brodawel-aberdovey.co.uk – £38-£65. Two minutes walk from the beach; views of golf course, Cardigan Bay. Interior features cottage-style breakfast room in calm, understated colours. Bedrooms have similar feel. Neat dining room; proud home cooking.

BARMOUTH

Fronoleu Hall, Llanaber, LL42 1YT, ☎ 01341 280491; kmbonser@fronoleu-hall.com – £75-£120. Late 19C house with striking view over Cardigan Bay. Well appointed guest lounge with tasteful country house feel. Sumptuous, stylish rooms boast an individualistic flair. Smart, cloth-clad dining room; local produce to the fore.

Llwyndû Farmhouse, LL42 1RR, ☎ 01341 280144; intouch@llwyndu-farmhouse.co.uk – £44-£80. Characterful part 17C farmhouse and 18C barn conversion on a hillside overlooking Cardigan Bay. Bunk beds and four-posters amidst stone walls and wood beams. An eclectic style of home-cooking using traditional regional ingredients.

BEAUMARIS

Ye Olde Bull's Head Inn, Castle St, LL58 8AP, ☎ 01248 810329; info@bullsheadinn.co.uk – £67-£120. Part 17C inn on the high street. Cosy pubby bar area sets the tone with period charm, brasses and bric-a-brac. Well decorated bedrooms, named after Dickens characters. Less formal dining facility decorated in an attractive modern style.

Mountfield, LL58 8RA, ☎ 01248 810380; – £50-£60. Set prominently at north end of seafront. Lead lined windows and neat garden. Combined lounge/breakfast room. Very pleasant bedrooms with views to castle and coastline.

BEDDGELERT

Sygun Fawr Country House, LL55 4NE, ☎ 01766 890258; sygunfawr@aol.com – £49-£68. Part 16C stone built house in Gwynant Valley. Superbly located, an elevated spot which affords exceptional views of Snowdon, particularly from double deluxe rooms. Simple dining room decorated in country style.

BENLLECH

Hafod, Amlwch Rd, LL74 8SR, ☏ 01248 853092; hughastley@amserve.net – £35-£50. Detached house with garden and some views of sea and bays. Well renovated and furnished to a good standard. Comfortably finished bedrooms well maintained by charming owner.

BETWS-Y-COED

Tan-y-Foel Country House, LL26 0RE, ☏ 01690 710507; enquiries@tyfhotel.co.uk – £99-£136. Part 16C country house, stylishly decorated in modern vein. Stunning views of Vale of Conwy and Snowdonia. Lovely rooms revel in the quality and elegance of the establishment. Rear room and conservatory make up the restaurant.

Llannerch Goch, Capel Garmon, LL26 0RL, ☏ 01690 710261; – £35-£56. Very peaceful 17C country house with original features. Pleasant sun lounge overlooking the garden. Set in four idyllic acres. Cosy sitting room, smart bedrooms.

Penmachno Hall, Penmachno, LL24 0PU, ☏ 01690 760410; enquiries@penmachnohall.co.uk – £58-£70. Former rectory built in 1862 with neat garden; super country setting. Sunny morning room where breakfast is served. Modern, bright bedrooms personally styled by the owners. Tasty home-cooking in deep burgundy communal dining room.

COLWYN BAY

Plas Rhos, Cayley Promenade, Rhos-on-Sea, LL28 4EP, ☏ 01492 543698; info@plasrhos.co.uk – £34-£76. 19C house on the first promenade from Colwyn Bay. Homely front lounge with bay view and fresh flowers. Breakfasts feature local butcher's produce. Immaculately kept rooms.

CONWY

Sychnant Pass House, Sychnant Pass Rd, LL32 8BJ, ☏ 01492 596868; bresykes@sychnant-pass-house.co.uk – £50-£90. Country house with Snowdonia National Park providing utterly peaceful backdrop. Charming sitting room with attractive décor. Comfy rooms, named after cats from T.S. Elliott. Informal dining room with bright lighting and seasonal menus.

Crows Nest Hall, LL32 8AZ, ☏ 01492 572956; tomandviv@crowsnesthall.co.uk – £45-£65. Over 150 years old, in three acres of gardens with delightful pond. Comfy sitting room in autumnal shades. Plenty of choice at breakfast. Individually appointed rooms.

Old Rectory Country House, Llanrwst Rd, Llansanffraid Glan Conwy, LL28 5LF, ☏ 01492 580611; info@oldrectorycountryhouse.co.uk – £99-£169. Enjoys fine position on Conwy Estuary; once home to parish rectors, renovated in Georgian style. House motto: «beautiful haven of peace»; antique beds, watercolours abound. Formal, antique furnished dining room serves accomplished set dinners.

DOLGELLAU

Abergwynant Hall, Penmaenpool, LL40 1YF, ☎ 01341 422160; relax@abergwynant.co.uk – £98-£150. For a memorable and peaceful stay, this grey stone Victorian mansion in sweeping grassland is particularly striking: unusual murals, antiques, individually themed bedrooms. A sunny restaurant with conservatory.

Tyddyn Mawr, Islawdref, Cader Rd, LL40 1TL, ☎ 01341 422331; – £40-£54. Part 18C farmhouse with sympathetic extension: boasts spectacular views from breathtaking position. Timbered breakfast room. Superb rooms: one with patio, one with balcony.

HARLECH

Hafod Wen, LL46 2RA, ☎ 01766 780356; enquiries@harlechguesthouse.co.uk – £36-£78. Unusual house with Dutch colonial architectural references. Superb views of Tremadoc Bay and Snowdonia from most of the antique and curio filled bedrooms. Footpath to beach. The dining room shares in the establishment's delightful views.

Gwrach Ynys, LL47 6TS, ☎ 01766 780742; info@gwrachynys.co.uk – £24-£58. Edwardian house in good location for exploring Snowdonia and Cardigan Bay. Welcoming owner. Traditional bedrooms, two of which are ideal for families.

HOLYHEAD

Yr Hendre, Porth-y-Felin Rd, LL65 1AH, ☎ 01407 762929; rita@yrhendre.freeserve.co.uk – £35-£55. Detached house dating from the 1920s in a pleasant, residential area of town and ideally located for the ferry terminus. Comfortable and well-furnished bedrooms. Breakfast overlooking the garden and with views of the sea.

LLANBEDR

Pensarn Hall, LL45 2HS, ☎ 01341 241236; welcome@pensarn-hall.co.uk – £35-£70. Late 19C house on an estuary. Impressive staircase and entrance with orginal tiled floor. Pleasant front conservatory. Breakfast room has good view. Large, well-kept rooms.

LLANDUDNO

Lympley Lodge, Colwyn Rd, Craigside, LL30 3AL, ☎ 01492 549304; enquiries@lympleylodge.co.uk – £40-£60. Charmingly run Victorian gentleman's residence in castellated style. A fine dining room for breakfasts. Rich bedrooms with a baroque tone and objets d'art. Murals abound.

Abbey Lodge, 14 Abbey Rd, LL30 2EA, ☎ 01492 878042; enquiries@abbeylodgeuk.com – £45-£75. Built as a gentlemen's residence in 1870; a pretty, gabled house with terraced garden and run by accommodating owners. Smart drawing room and cosy, comfortable bedrooms. Dine «en famille» around a communal table with lace cover and carved chairs.

Epperstone, 15 Abbey Rd, LL30 2EE, ☏ 01492 878746; epperstonehotel@btconnect.com – £33-£66. A period house, evident in the fixtures: stained glass, ornate fireplace, mahogany staircase. Other attractions include a marine aquarium in conservatory and neat bedrooms. Intimate dining room serving varied dishes using fresh, local ingredients.

Cranberry House, 12 Abbey Rd, LL30 2EA, ☏ 01492 879760; cranberryhse@aol.com – £35-£54. A white, bay windowed Victorian house boasting an immaculate style; pretty garden outside, tastefully furnished inside with fine quality fabrics in bedrooms.

Craiglands House, 7 Carmen Sylva Rd, LL30 1LZ, ☏ 01492 875090; enq@craiglandsllandudno.co.uk – £20-£60. Situated off the promenade, within walking distance of the town; run by convivial owner. Rooms are individually styled; the perfect place for forays into the countryside. Four course menus of simple, no-frills homecooking.

LLANEGRYN

Peniarth Uchaf, LL36 9UG, ☏ 01654 710804; corbett@birdrock.co.uk – £40-£84. 18C house in four acres of woodland. Beautiful drawing room boasts log fire and antiques. Family home style rooms with private bathrooms: one has full working Victorian bath. Fine dining room with period feel: country meals on offer.

LLANERCHYMEDD

Llwydiarth Fawr, LL71 8DF, ☏ 01248 470321; llwydiarth@hotmail.com – £35-£60. Part of a 1000-acre cattle and sheep farm, Georgian in style with picturesque country vistas. Guests can enjoy nature walks, fishing on lake; welcoming owner. Well-kept rooms.

Drws-Y-Coed, LL71 8AD, ☏ 01248 470473; drws.ycoed@virgin.net – £35-£52. Meaning «Door of the Wood»; run by Welsh speaking family in 550-acre farm of cattle and cereal crops. Original buildings have been preserved whilst bedrooms are trim, tidy.

LLAN FFESTINIOG

Cae'r Blaidd Country House, LL41 4PH, ☏ 01766 762765; info@caerblaidd.fsnet.co.uk – £40-£64. Spacious Victorian country house in wooded gardens; spectacular views of Ffestiniog and Moelwyn Mountains. Smart, uncluttered rooms. Guided tours and courses are organised. A huge dining room; large refectory table where communal dinners are served.

Tyddyn du Farm, Gellilydan, LL41 4RB, ☏ 01766 590281; mich/paula@snowdoniafarm.com – £40-£85. 400-year old farmhouse set against Moelwyn Mountains. Guests can participate in farming activities or visit Roman site. Bedrooms have large jacuzzis. Minimum two night stay. Cooking takes in free-range farm eggs; soups and rolls are homemade.

LLANGOLLEN

Oakmere, Regent St, LL20 8HS, ☏ 01978 861126; oakmeregh@aol.com – £38-£55. A restored Victorian house with terraced garden, all weather tennis court. Indoors are polished pitch pine furnishings and tidy bedrooms.

MENAI BRIDGE

Wern Farm, Pentraeth Rd, LL59 5RR, ☏ 01248 712421; wernfarmanglesey@onetel.net.uk – £55-£70. Attractive Georgian farmhouse run by a friendly couple. Bedrooms are spacious and comfortable. Enjoy countryside views in conservatory where vast breakfast is offered.

PWLLHELI

The Old Rectory, Boduan, LL53 6DT, ☏ 01758 721519; thepollards@theoldrectory.net – £50-£80. Part Georgian house with garden and paddock, adjacent to church. Well restored providing comfortable, individually decorated bedrooms and attractive sitting room. Dining room decorated in keeping with the age and atmosphere of the house.

RUTHIN

Ye Olde Anchor Inn, Rhos St, LL15 1DY, ☏ 01824 702813; hotel@anchorinn.co.uk – £40-£60. Part 18C inn in the centre of the village. Personally run with a cosy atmosphere epitomised in the snug bar with its beams and brasses. Comfortable, uniform bedrooms. Light menu in the bar and fuller meals in the traditionally appointed restaurant.

Firgrove, Llanfwrog, LL15 2LL, ☏ 01824 702677; meadway@firgrovecountryhouse.co.uk – £45-£70. A well-furnished house with tasteful interiors set within attractive gardens. Bedrooms are comfortable and one is self-contained with a small kitchen. Close to the town. Traditionally furnished dining room with meals taken at a communal table.

Eyarth Station, Llanfair Dyffryn Clwyd, LL15 2EE, ☏ 01824 703643; stay@eyarthstation.com – £35-£54. Former railway station with a fine collection of photographs of its previous life. Pleasant country location. Traditional décor in bedrooms, sitting room and a small bar. Views over the countryside and hearty home-cooked food in the dining room.

TREMEIRCHION

Bach-Y-Graig, LL17 0UH, ☏ 01745 730627; anwen@bachygraig.co.uk – £35-£54. Attractive brick-built farmhouse dating from 16C, on working farm. In quiet spot with woodland trails nearby. Large open fires and pine furnished rooms with cast iron beds.

■ Restaurants ■

The two prices given for each establishment represent a minimum and maximum price for a full meal excluding beverages.

BEAUMARIS

The Restaurant, Castle St, LL58 8AP, ☏ (01248) 810329; £30-£33. In contrast to the inn the restaurant has a contemporary feel and style engendered by subtle colours and modern lighting. A fresh approach to traditional ingredients.

COLWYN BAY

Pen-y-Bryn, Pen-y-Bryn Rd, Upper Colwyn Bay, LL29 6DD, ☏ (01492) 533360; pen.y.bryn@brunningandprice.co.uk – £15-£21. Built in the 1970s, with sloped garden and bay view. Spacious interior with large, polished wood tables. Extensive menus feature Welsh dishes with eclectic influences.

HARLECH

Castle Cottage, Pen Llech, LL46 2YL, ☏ (01766) 780479; glyn@castlec ottageharlech.co.uk – £25. A little cottage just a short distance from the imposing Harlech Castle. Snug, beamed dining room where Welsh food with a modern twist is served. Compact, cosy bedrooms (£58-£130).

HAWARDEN

The Brasserie, 68 The Highway, CH5 3DH, ☏ (01244) 536353 – £17-£23. Neutral walls, wood floors and spot lighting contribute to the busy, modern ambience in this good value, small restaurant; well reputed locally. Cuisine with a Welsh tone.

LLANBERIS

Y Bistro, 43-45 High St, LL55 4EU, ☏ (01286) 871278; ybistro@fsbdial.co.uk – £24-£32. Long established, in lakeside village at foot of Snowdonia. Brush up on your Welsh when perusing menus of Eidion Badell (beef flamed in Cognac), Cawl Tomato Ceiros, (soup).

LLANDUDNO

Osborne's Cafe Grill, 17 North Parade, LL30 2LP, ☏ (01492) 860330 – £22-£32. Luxurious, opulent main dining room with velvet drapes and ornate gold lighting. Eclectic, modern menus, enthusiastic service. Also, grill bar and conservatory options.

LLANDUDNO

Richard's Bistro, 7 Church Walks, LL30 2HD, ☏ (01492) 875315; richa rdhendey@supanet.com – £24. A cosy, cellar-like bistro in town centre – stone walls and floor, simple wooden tables. A range of Welsh and British dishes which might include black pudding with grapes.

Queens Head, Glanwydden, LL31 9JP, ☎ (01492) 546570; enquiries@queensheadglanwydden.co.uk – £15-£21. Popular pub which is renowned for its imaginative, weekly changing bar menus. The creative dishes are served in a modern lounge of smart black tables.

Sands Brasserie, 59-63 Station Rd, Deganwy, LL31 9DF, ☎ (01492) 592659 – £18-£22. Modern brasserie with deep blue/green walls and halogen lights along metal wires. Warm, informal service of well-priced, eclectic dishes utilising global influences.

Nikki Ip's, 57 Station Rd, Deganwy, LL31 9DF, ☎ (01492) 596611 – £18-£30. Good value, stylish and unconventional, but beware: no signage outside. Particularly welcoming owners. Coral interior; Cantonese, Peking and Szechuan specialities are served.

✗**Paysanne**, Station Rd, Deganwy, LL31 9EJ, ☎ (01492) 582079 – £20. Neat restaurant with a friendly ambience; Welsh and mainly French fare offered. There is a good selection of local fish and a carefully sourced French wine list.

LLANGOLLEN

The Corn Mill, Dee Lane, LL20 8PN, ☎ (01978) 869555; corn-mill@brunningandprice.co.uk – £17-£22. Imposing corn mill on banks of the Dee with large decked seating area extending into the river. Inside are two restored water wheels, slate and brick rooms. Rustic cuisine.

MENAI BRIDGE

Ruby, Dale St, LL59 5AW, ☎ (01248) 714999; rubymenai@aol.com – £11-£21 £29. Former firestation and council offices; now a lively, bustling eatery on two floors with good local reputation. Eclectic, global menus employing flavoursome, vibrant cooking.

MOLD

The Stables, CH7 6AB, ☎ (01352) 840577; info@soughtonhall.co.uk – £22-£28. Walk through the grounds to a 17C stable block; bar and first-floor brasserie in bare brick and scrubbed pine. Tasty classics from an open kitchen. Terrace for summer lunch.

Glas Fryn, Raikes Lane, Sychdyn, CH7 6LR, ☎ (01352) 750500; glasfryn@brunningandprice.co.uk – £16-£21. Informal and open-plan; sepia prints, crammed bookshelves and rows of old bottles surround wooden tables. Varied brasserie menu draws a lively young set.

WREXHAM

Pant-yr-Ochain, Old Wrexham Rd, Gresford, LL12 8TY, ☎ (01978) 853525; pant.yr.ochain@brunningandprice.co.uk – £18. Bustling part 16C inn overlooking a lake with pleasant gardens and terrace. Open-plan dining rooms, bar and library. Blackboard menu and real ales.

■ What to buy locally ■

Craftwork is a living tradition in Wales; in craft centres all over the country skilled men and women demonstrate their talents and sell their products. Many museums also have demonstrations of traditional crafts.

Wales – A Touring Guide to Crafts is published by the Wales Tourist Board; local Tourist Information Centres provide information about their own areas.

The crafts practised include fashion garments, glass-blowing, jewellery, pewter work, pottery, slate work, weaving and wood-turning.

Apart from providing sweet Welsh lamb for the table, the many sheep on the hillsides provide wool which is woven into a variety of **woollen goods** – there are mills in most parts of the country.

The **slate** which provides roofs and fences is also made into commemorative plaques and other objects of beauty.

Local glass manufacturers produce **glassware** with typical Welsh designs.

Wooden articles from furniture to a simple salad bowl are hand-turned on the lathe or various types of wood are carved into the elaborate Welsh lovespoons.

■ Visiting ■

CADW – The organisation, whose name means "To protect", manages 131 ancient monuments, including many castles, in all parts of Wales. Visitors from abroad, who intend to visit more than a small number of CADW properties, should consider becoming members of CADW or of English Heritage, whose members have visiting rights.

CADW: Welsh Historic Monuments, Crown Building, Cathays Park, Cardiff CF10 3NQ. ☎ 029 2050 0200; Fax 029 2082 6375; cadw@wales.gsi.gov.uk; www.cadw.wales.gov.uk

National Parks – Wales has three national parks – Snowdonia, the Brecon Beacons and Pembrokeshire Coast – which offer many opportunities for outdoor activities and sports (walking, rambling), and some forests, which are managed with recreation in mind.

Nature Reserves – Wales has many nature reserves, some with birdwatching centres, both on the coast and inland where great efforts have been made to re-establish the red kite in its native habitat.

Tourist Railways – The many different scenic and tourist lines, some operated by steam engines, are marketed together as **Great Little Trains of Wales**. A **Wanderer Ticket** is available valid for unlimited travel during any 8 days within a 15 day period or any 4 days within an 8 day period on all eight **Great Little Trains** – Bala Lake Railway *(see p 25)*, Ffestiniog Railway *(see p 34)*, Llanberis Lake Railway *(see p 61)*, Talyllyn Railway *(see p 103)*, Welsh Highland Railway *(see p 85)* and Welshpool and Llanfair Light Railway.

Music – Wales has a long tradition and widespread reputation for music, particularly the human voice, and poetry.

The **Welsh Male Voice Choirs**, of which there are over 60, usually admit members of the public to their rehearsals. A booklet giving rehearsal locations and times, and the names, addresses and telephone numbers of contacts – *Welsh Male Voice Choirs (Corau Meibion Cymru)* – is available from the Wales Tourist Board *(see p 110)* or from local Tourist Information Centres.

The **International Musical Eisteddfod**, held in Llangollen annually in early July (5 days), offers performances by male voice choirs, female choirs, mixed choirs, folk song groups, children's choirs, solo singers and of opera.

The **National Eisteddfod of Wales**, which is held annually in August (9 days), in North Wales and South Wales in alternate years, promotes the Welsh language through a Welsh cultural fair; Welsh dancing, music and poetry recitations in the Bardic tradition take place in the Main Pavilion, while the satellites provide concerts, plays, arts and crafts and science exhibitions.

■ Sport ■

Rambling – Wales is a walker's paradise, with a dense network of rights of way and exhilarating mountain and coastal paths. There are two national trails and several waymarked long-distance routes. There are also many trails in nature reserves and forests.

Mountain Biking and Climbing – Centres for hiring and using mountain bikes and quad bikes are fairly numerous.

Snowdonia *(see p 94)* is one of the cradles of British mountaineering where serious climbers spend time in training for their attempts at greater things, such as the conquest of Everest.

Mountain walkers should bear in mind that temperatures drop rapidly as height is gained, roughly by 2 C for every 1 000ft/300m. This, combined with wind-chill, means that summit conditions can be unpleasantly, even dangerously, different from those which seemed so encouraging at the starting point of a climb in the valley bottom.

Golf – Details of the more than 160 golf courses in Wales are given in the Wales Tourist Board's comprehensive brochure *Golfing in Wales*. Many are listed in the **Michelin Red Guide Great Britain and Ireland**. Most are privately owned and accept visitors. Municipal courses are usually very heavily used, with long queues at the first tee.

Cycling – Much of Wales is ideal mountain biking country, and there are also combined cycling and walking routes like the Taff Trail leading north from Cardiff into the South Wales Valleys. A Cycle Network is being established so that Wales can be crossed by bicycle from north to south and east to west; these routes are part of the National Cycle Network covering the whole of Britain comprising 5 000mi/8 000km of traffic-free routes and traffic-calmed and minor roads. For information apply to

Cycles are available for hire from a number of centres. The Wales Tourist Board brochure *Cycling Wales* gives full details.

Fishing – Wales offers fishing in the lakes and reservoirs and along the coast. There is also the possibility of deep-sea fishing from a limited number of harbours. The Wye and Usk are famous for salmon fishing; Llyn Brenig is preserved exclusively for fly-fishing.

A leaflet on fishing the reservoirs of Wales, giving information on dates, times, permits, charges and facilities for the disabled, is published by the Welsh Water Authority.

Sailing – There are many opportunities for sailing at sea off the long and varied coastline of Wales, in the many estuaries and inland on the lakes and reservoirs (dinghy sailing on Bala Lake and Llangorse Lake). Some of the best sailing is to be found off the Lleyn Peninsula.

■ Further reading ■

For reference...

Artists in Snowdonia by James Bogle (Y Lolfa Cyf, 1990)

Wild Wales by George Borrow (Bridge, 2002)

A History of Wales by John Davies (Penguin, 1994)

Historic Architecture of Wales by John B Hilling (University of Wales Press, 1976)

A History of Modern Wales 1536-1990 by Philip Jenkins (Longman, 1991)

The Matter of Wales: Epic Views of a Small Country by Jan Morris (Penguin, 1986)

Wales from the Air by Chris Musson (Ebury, 2001)

Wales: An Anthology ed by Alice Thomas Ellis (Fontana, 1991)

When Was Wales?: A History of the Welsh by Gwyn A Williams (Penguin, 1985)

For pleasure...

On the Black Hill by Bruce Chatwin (Vintage, 1998)

Clough Williams-Ellis: Architect of Portmeirion by Jonah Jones (Seron, 1998)

How Green Was My Valley by Richard Llewellyn (Penguin, 2001)

Dylan: Fern Hill to Milk Wood by David Rowe (Gomer Press, 1999)

Collected Stories by Dylan Thomas (Phoenix, 2000)

Clouds of Time and other stories by John E Williams (Gwasg Carreg Gwalch, 1999)

■ Calendar of events ■

1 March
Throughout Wales St David's Day: celebrated all over the country, with special services in St David's Cathedral

March
Llangollen Jazz festival
Wrexham Arts festival

Late May–end December
Throughout Wales Mid-Wales festival of the Countryside – over 500 events such as birdwatching, guided walks, arts and crafts, sheepdog trials, farm and garden visits

Late May–early June
Beaumaris Arts festival and regatta, Beaumaris, Anglesey
Variable location The Urdd National (Welsh League of Youth) Eisteddfod, one of the largest youth festivals in Europe

July
Llanfyllin Annual Music Festival

Mid-July
Llangollen International Musical *Eisteddfod* (5 days)

Late July
Builth Wells Royal Welsh Agricultural Show

August
Llanfyllin Annual Agricultural Show
Denbigh Denbigh and Flint Show

Early August
Variable location Royal National Eisteddfod of Wales (9 days)

Late August (1 week)
Llandrindod Wells Llandrindod Wells Victorian Festival – street theatre, drama, exhibitions, walks, talks and music – all with a Victorian flavour

Last full week of August
Machynlleth Arts Festival

Late August to early September
Presteigne Festival of Music and the Arts

Last full week of September
St Asaph North Wales Music Festival

INDEX

A

Aberconwy Centre 63
Aberdaron 76
Abersoch 74
Acts of Union 11
Alice in Wonderland Centre 64
Alternative Technology Centre ... 78
Anglesey 20, 82
Aqueduct 50
   Pont-Cysyllte 71
Art gallery 36, 74
Augustine, Saint 10

B

Bala Lake 25
Barclodiad y Gawres 22, 24
Bardsey Island 76
Barmouth 28
Beaker People 7
Beaumaris 30
Berwyn Mountains 66
Bethesda 100
Betws-y-Coed 32
Bevan, Aneurin 14
Birdwatching ... 50, 72, 75, 77, 119
Blaenau Ffestiniog 34, 85
Bodnant Garden 37
Bodelwyddan 36
Brecon 10
Bridge
   Mena 21
Britannia Bridge 21
Brittonic 7
Bronze Age 6
Bryn-Celli-Ddu 21
Burial chamber 21, 22, 24
Butler, Lady Eleanor 83
Bwlch y Groes 25

C

Caban Coch Dam 49
Cadair Idris 47, 102
Cadfan, Saint 103
Caerleon 10
Caernarfon 10, 38
Caerphilly cheese 17
Cambrian Woollen Mill 72
Canal Exhibition Centre 71
Canal
   Ellesmere 71
   Montgomery 106
   Shropshire Union 69
Canoeing 67
Capel Curig 101
Carnedd range 98
Castell Dinas Brân 70
Castle of the Winds 101
Castle
   Beaumaris 30
   Bodelwyddan 36
   Caernarfon 38
   Cardiff 13
   Castell Dinas Brân 70
   Chirk 41
   Conwy 44
   Denbigh 46
   Harlech 54
   Penrhyn 13, 81
   Powis 88
   Rhuddlan 91
Cathedral
   Bangor 26
   St Asaph 93
Celtica 78
Celtic language 78
Celtic people 7, 78
Cemaes 24
Centre for Alternative
   Technology 78
Chapel
   St Trillo's, Colwyn Bay 42
Charles, Thomas 12
Chartists 13
Chester 10
Chirk 41

Church
- Llanbadrig 24
- St Cadfan's, Tywyn 103
- St David's, Newtown 80
- St Mary's, Betws-y-Coed 33
- St Mary's, Newtown 80
- St Michael's, Betws-y-Coed ... 33

Cistercian 43, 104
Claerwen Dam 50
Clive, Edward 88
Clogwyn Station 61
Clwyd, River 91, 92
Clwyd, Vale of 46
Cnicht 95
Coal 13, 107
Conwy, River 32, 43
Conwy 43
Copper 12, 60
Corris Craft Centre 78
Country Park
- Padarn 60

Cox, David 33
Craft 78, 86
- Cambrian Woollen Mill 72

Cregennen Lakes 102
Crib Goch 97
Cwm Idwal 101
Cybi, Saint 56
Cymdeithas yr Iaith Gymraeg ... 15
Cymry 10

D

Dam 48, 105
David, Saint 10
Dee, River 66
Deheubarth 11
Deiniol, Saint 26
Denbigh 46
Deva 10
Devil's Kitchen 101
Devolution 15
Dewi Sant 10
Dinas Oleu 29
Dinorwig Quarry 60
Disestablishment 14
Dol-y-Mynach Dam 50
Dolgellau 47

Dovey, River 78, 103
Drovers 72
Dulas, River 78
Dwyryd, River 86, 95
Dyfi, River 78
Dysynni, River 103

E

Education 14
Edwards, Owen M. 14
Edward II 40
Edward I 30, 38, 41, 43,
                   46, 54, 88, 91
Eglwyseg, River 104
Eisteddfod 66, 69
Elan, River 49
Elan Valley 48
Elan Village 49
Elwy, River 93
Erch, River 74
Erddig 51

F - G

Fairbourne 28
Ffestiniog, Vale of 85, 95
Ffridd Faldwyn 79
Fish Forest 23
Folklore 70
Gaer, Y 10
Garden 75
- Bodnant 37
- Erddig 53
- Plas Tan-y-Bwlch 95
- Powis Castle 90

Garreg-ddu Dam 50
Glaciation 95
Glaciers 95
Gladstone,
  William Ewart 27, 97, 100
Glaslyn, River 84
Glyders, The 101
Glyn Dŵr, Owain ....
      .... 26, 31, 39, 55, 78, 104
Goch, River 100
Golf 120
Great Orme, The 65

Great Orme cable car 65
Gruffudd ap
    Gwynwynwyn.................88, 106

H - I - J

Hansom, J A 30, 36
Harlech 54
Harris, Howel 12
Haven Holiday Park 73
Henry VII 11
Hen Domen 79
Herbert, Sir Edward 88
Holyhead 56
Hopper, Thomas 81
Hywel Dda 11
Industry 12
Irfon, River 72
Iron-Age fort 71, 79, 100
Ironworking 13
Isca 10
James of St George, Master......30,
        39, 41, 43, 45, 55, 91

K - L

Keating family 75
Kentigern, Saint 93
Knighton 58
Lake 25, 60, 105
Lifeboat Museum 28
Llanbadrig 24
Llanbedrog 74
Llanberis Path 97
Llanberis 60
Llandudno 62
Llanfairpwllgwyngyll 21
Llanfair Hill 59
Llangefni 22
Llangollen, Ladies of 67, 83
Llangollen, Vale of 66
Llangollen 66, 83
Llanwrtyd Wells 72
Llechwedd Slate Caverns 35
Lleyn Peninsula 73
Lloyd George, David 13
Llyn Cau 102
Llyn Idwal 101
Llyn Ogwen 101
Llyn Padarn 60

Llyn Tegid 25
Llywelyn the Great 104
Llywelyn the Last 22

M

Mabinogion 55
Machynlleth 78
Macsen Wledig 10
Madocks, William 84
Madog ap Llywelyn 39, 46, 55
Magnus Maximus 10
Male voice choirs 120
Marches, The 6
Mawddach estuary 47
Menai Strait 21
Methodism 12
Minfordd Path 102
Missionaries 10
Moel Hebog 95
Moel Siabod 101
Monastery 104
Monastic 43, 76, 93
Montgomery 79
Morgan, William 12
Mortimer, Roger 41
Mostyn family 62
Motoring 111
Mountain Centre 96, 101
Mungo, Saint 93
Museum
    Barmouth 28
    Betws Motor 33
    Canal 71
    Celtica 78
    Clive 90
    Conwy Valley Railway 33
    Ffestiniog Railway 85
    Lifeboat 28
    Llangollen Motor 71
    Maritime (Holyhead) 57
    Maritime (Porthmadog) 84
    Oriel Ynys Môn 22
    Porthmadog Maritime 84
    Robert Owen Memorial 80
    Talyllyn Railway 103
    Victorian School 69
    Welsh Slate 60
Music 70, 120

Mwnt 76
Myddelton, Thomas 41
Mynydd Enlli 76
Mynydd Eppynt 72
Mynydd Mawr 77

N

Nant Ffrancon 100
Nationalism 14
National Mountain
  Centre 96, 101
National Park
  Snowdonia 32, 94
National Portrait Gallery 36
Nature Reserves 119
Nature Reserve
  Bardsey Island 77
  Cwm Idwal 101
Newtown 80
Normans 11

O - P

Offa's Dyke 10, 58
Ogwen Cottage 101
Ogwen, River 100
Oriel Ynys Môn 22
Owen, Robert 80
Padarn Country Park 60
Patrick, Saint 24
Pembroke, Earl of 88
Penarth Fawr 73
Penmaen Mawr 100
Pennant family 81
Penrhyn Quarries 81, 100
Penrhyn 81
Pen-y-Gaer 100
Pier 27, 30, 63
Plaid Cymru 14
Plas-yn-Rhiw 75
Plas Glyn-y-Weddw 74
Plas Halt 85
Plas Mawr 45
Plas Newydd 82, 83
Plas Tan-y-Bwlch 85, 95

Plas y Brenin 101
Ponsonby, Sarah 83
Pont Cysyllte 71
Pont-y-Pair 32
Porthmadog 34, 84
Porth Dinllaen 77
Portmeirion 86
Pottery 86
Power Station
  Tan-y-Grisiau 85
  Wylfa 24
Powis Castle 88
Powys County Observatory 59
Precipice Walk 47, 102
Prince of Wales 57, 78
Pwllheli 73

Q - R

Quarries 34, 60, 81
Railway 119
  Bala Lake 25
  Fairbourne 28
  Ffestiniog 34, 84
  Llanberis Lake 61
  Llangollen 68
  Snowdon Mountain 61, 97
  Spiral 85
  Talyllyn 103
  Welsh Highland 85
Rebecca Rioters 13
Red kite 72
Reformation 12
Religion 12, 78
Repton, Humphry 82
Reservoir 48, 85, 105
Rhodri Mawr 10
Rhos-on-Sea 42
Rhyl 92
Rifiera Gymreig, Y 74
Ririd Flaidd 41
Riviera, Welsh 74
Roman 7, 56
Rowland, Daniel 12
Royal International Pavilion 69
Ruskin, John 29

S

Sailing 25, 121
Sail boarding 25
St Tudwal's Islands 75
Sand dunes................................. 102
Scott, Sir Gilbert 93, 104
Scott, Sir Walter 67
Scouse...79
Seals......................................75, 77
Segontium 10
Severn, River 79
Shelley, Percy Bysshe 49, 67
Shopping...................................... 119
Slate...............................12, 34, 60,
81, 84, 95, 100
Snowdonia National Park
    Information Centre 103
Snowdonia National Park Visitor
    Centre 32, 34, 47, 54
Snowdonia 6, 94
Snowdon 95
Southey, Robert............................67
Spa 72
Stephenson, Robert.....................21
Stone Age... 6

T - U - V

Talbot, Fanny..................................29
Tan-y-Grisiau 85
Taste of Wales...............................17
Television.......................................16
Telford, Thomas .. 21, 32, 56, 67
Tipu Sahib's tent............................90
Tourism..16
Town walls.....................................45
Tregaron 72
Tryfan.. 101
Tudor 11
Tywyn... 103

Ucheldre Centre 57
Union, Acts of 11
University.............................. 14, 27
Urdd Gobaith Cymru 14
Valle Crucis Abbey..................... 104
Victorian School...........................69
Vikings...10
Vyrnwy, Lake 105

W - Y - Z

Waterfall
    Aber 100
    Horseshoe Falls 69
Watersports..................................25
Welsh Assembly 15
Welshpool................................... 106
Welsh Development
    Agency 15, 16
Welsh language...........11, 15, 16,
20, 27, 57
Welsh Mountain Zoo...................42
Welsh Nationalist Party 14
Welsh Not.....................................57
Welsh Office 15
Welsh Riviera...............................74
What to Buy 119
Whistler, Rex 82
Williams-Ellis,
    Sir Clough 64, 76, 86
Williams, Sir William....................36
Windsurfing..................................25
Wnion, River 47
Wordsworth, William..................67
Wrexham.................................... 107
Wyddfa, Yr 95
Wylfa Nuclear Power Station ...24
Ynys Enlli......................................76
Yorke family.................................51
Zoo
    Anglesey Sea 23
    Welsh Mountain..........................42

Director	David Brabis
Series Editor	Mike Brammer
Editor	Alison Hughes
Picture Editor	Geneviève Corbic, Éliane Bailly
Mapping	Michèle Cana, Alain Baldet
Graphics Coordination	Marie-Pierre Renier
Graphics	Antoine Diemoz-Rosset
Lay-out	Alain Fossé
Typesetting	Sophie Rassel and Franck Malagie (NORDCOMPO)
Production	Renaud Leblanc
Marketing	Cécile Petiau, Hervé Binétruy
Sales	John Lewis (UK), Robin Bird (USA)
Public Relations	Gonzague de Jarnac, Paul Cordle
Special Thanks:	Jon Combe
Contact	Michelin Travel Publications Hannay House 39 Clarendon Road Watford Herts WD17 1JA United Kingdom ☏ (01923) 205 240 Fax (01923) 205 241 www.ViaMichelin.com TheGreenGuide-uk@uk.michelin.com

Hannay House, 39 Clarendon Road.
Watford, Herts WD17 1JA, UK
www.ViaMichelin.com
TheGreenGuide-uk@uk.michelin.com

MANUFACTURE FRANÇAISE DES PNEUMATIQUES MICHELIN
Société en commandite par actions au capital de 304 000 000 EUR
Place des Carmes-Déchaux – 63 Clermont-Ferrand (France)
R.C.S. Clermont-Fd B 855 200 507

No part of this publication may be reproduced in any form
without the prior permission of the publisher

© Michelin et Cie, propriétaires-éditeurs
Dépôt légal juin 2004
Printed in France 05.04/1.1
Impression : IME, Baume-les-Dames

Published in 2004